KNOW YOUR SPIRITUAL IDENTITY

"Jesus answered and said unto him, Verily, verily,
I say unto thee, Except a man be born again,
he cannot see the kingdom of God."

John 3:3

By
David A. Olaniyan

Know Your Spiritual Identity
COPYRIGHT© 2019 By David A Olaniyan
ISBN: 978-1-732-743-70-0

All right reserved. This book or any portion thereof may not be reproduced or used in any manner whatsoever without the express written permission of the publisher, except for the use of brief quotations in a book review.
All Bible quotes are from King James Version and others as noted.

Published by:
Jesus Witness Ministries Inc Publishing House
---a k a JWM. A Publication arm of Jesus Witness Ministries Inc.

"That I may publish with the voice of thanksgiving and tell of all thy wondrous works."
Psalms 26:7

To order additional copies, wholesales or booking:
Call the Church office (973-902-8160)
Ministry Prayer-line 1-774-220-4000 code 6643177
Monday & Thursday 11am-1200noon.

Administrative Head Office Address & Worship Center:
2 Grove place East Orange New Jersey 07107 USA
Email: Jesuswitnessministries@gmail.com
Website: www.jesuswitnessministries.com

This book is a production of Jesus Witness Ministries Publishing House. A publication Arms of Jesus Witness Ministries 2019 First Edition

CONTENTS

Acknowledgement iv
Introduction 6
Mission 22
Chapter 1 Perversions 25
Chapter 2 What Does Bible History Show? 30
Chapter 3 Illicit Drugs and Alcohol 34
Chapter 4 Persecution of God's Children 38
Chapter 5 False Religion 40
Chapter 6 Endurance is Required for Salvation 45
Chapter 7 Gross Darkness Covered the People: ... 65
Chapter 8 You Shall Reap What You Sow 71
Chapter 9 God of Mercy and Discipline 75
Chapter 10 The Solutions to Identity Crisis 80
Chapter 11 The Importance of Finding One's Identity 86
Chapter 12 The Identity Keys That Break all Barriers 92
Chapter 13 Prayers of Deliverance 160
About The Ministry 172
About The Author 176

ACKNOWLEDGEMENT

I dedicate this book to my God, the father of all creation, *to Jesus Christ*, and to *the Holy Spirit* who inspired me to write this book.

I thank God for giving me the *grace of eternal life*. I thank Jesus for giving me *the power* and *the authority* to cast out demons and to heal the sick. I thank God for the *healing,* and *deliverance* anointing upon my life in a supernatural measure.

I thank *Akintokunbo Akinbowale* and *Rev. Franklin N. Abazie* for their dedication and assistance in designing, editing, and proofreading this book.

My sincere appreciation goes to my spiritual fathers, and coworkers in the evangelism work of soul winning for Christ Jesus. *"Those who win souls are wise",* the Bible says in (Proverb 11:30). I thank my

Acknowledgement

wife for her relentless sacrifice, patience, and endurance during the reproduction of this great book.

Know Your Spiritual Identity

INTRODUCTION

I wrote this book to *liberate people* who have been a victim of an *identity crisis.* So many people today need *deliverance from the wiles of the devil.*

In this end time, *evil oppression is manifesting* in a higher plat form. We see all kinds of immoralities, such as perversions, addictions, false religion, persecution of God's children and wickedness into the world.

Among other plans of the devil-is to depopulate the world through wars between opposing countries of the world. The devil is using *perversions, illicit drugs, alcohol abuse, persecution, and killing of innocent children of God.*

For example, besides *millions of people* losing their lives in any military war,

Introduction

millions of people are dying due to diseases and practices that God forbids.

The legalization of *sodomy* and *bestiality* as human rights can only catapult the number of the victim of identity crisis in God and the persecution of God's children to the highest heaven.

The new legislation in California forbids the sale of the Bible and prohibits people from reading any book that can deliver people from perversion. There is no doubt in my heart that this law persecutes the people of God.

How does God feel about these perversions, drugs and alcohol abuse?

In the past, God demonstrated his hatred for practices of *bestiality* and *sodomy* by exterminating the Canaanites, the Hittites, and the Jebusites. God allocated their land to the children of Israel.

Know Your Spiritual Identity

Can you accuse God of partiality?

The answer is no!

God warned those pagan nations of the consequences of their lewd behavior, but they refused to change. God said, *"You shall not lie with a male as with a woman. It is an abomination. Nor shall you mate with any animal, to defile yourself with it. Nor shall any woman stand before an animal to mate with it. It is a perversion. Do not defile yourselves with any of these things; for by all these the nations are defiled, which I am casting out before you. For the land is defiled; therefore I visit the punishment of its iniquity upon it, and the land vomits out its inhabitants. "You shall, therefore, keep My statutes and My judgments, and shall not commit any of these abominations, either any of your own nation or any stranger who dwells among you (for all these abominations the men of*

Introduction

the land have done, who were before you, and thus the land is defiled), lest the land vomit you out also when you defile it, as it vomited out the nations that were before you". For whoever commits any of these abominations, the persons who commit them shall be cut off from among their people." **(Leviticus 18:22-30)**

More also, the book of Genesis 19:24-25 describes how God destroyed *the cities of Sodom and Gomorrah* for *the practices of homosexuality*. Many nations including the United States of America prohibit *sodomy practices* until 2003 in a case called Lawrence v.Texas, the Supreme Court of the United States ruled that sodomy laws be unconstitutional.

This means no sodomy law in the United States can be used to charge a person with a crime. Recently India Supreme Court abrogated laws banning same-sex marriages. Even though Indian is not a Christian nation, yet they have a rule that forbids same-sex marriages until recently.

However, sodomy is still illegal in many African countries. Some of the countries that refused to adopt *homosexuality* as a way of life may have been denied economic prosperity by powerful nations. Sodomy has become the mark of the wild-beast.

"He causes all, both small and great, rich and poor, free and slave, to receive a mark on their right hand or on their foreheads, and that no one may buy or sell except one who has the mark or the name of the beast, or the number of his name".

Here is wisdom. Let him who has understanding calculate the number of the beast, for it is the number of a man: *His number is "666"*. **Revelation 13:16-17**.

The above Scriptures was fulfilled when official car of United States President Obama was code-named "The Beast" and

Introduction

when the Supreme Court legalized sodomy as a human right, and when president Obama went to many countries promoting LGBT as human rights.

Obama threatened many countries that refused to embrace *LGBT as human rights* with economic sanctions.

That country will not be able to buy nor sell without the mark of the wild beast. For example, America refused to sell military Equipment and provides other financial assistance to Nigeria to fight terrorist because they pass a law forbidden homosexuality among others.

God said,

"Woe to those who are saying that good is bad and bad is good, those who are putting darkness for light and light for darkness, those who are putting bitter for sweet and sweet for bitter! Woe to those wise

in their own eyes and discreet even in front of their own faces". **(Isaiah 5:20-21)**

Sin is Satan identification number. For example, a popular world news anchor was indulging him-self with nicotine for a long time and suddenly he was diagnosed with Lung Cancer and died.

Others may suffer from COPD-Chronic obstructive pulmonary disease. The *smokers usually end up in mortuary and grave. The Bible described sin as an employer that pays wages of sickness and death. "The wages of sin is death* **(Roman 6:23).**

It is my prayer that God will hear the cry of the believers in this troubled time of the end and save people out of their distress and confusion. "*He sent his word and healed them and delivers them from their destruction."* **(Psalm 107:20)**

I am convinced that if we know the purpose of God in our life, we will develop a

Introduction

personal relationship and fellowship with the Holy Spirit. This relationship and fellowship will help us identify with our root in Jesus Christ. We will then be *able to recognize the power and role of the Holy Spirit in our personal life*. The Holy Spirit-as the helper-helps us live according to the commandment of God.

God said, *"For I know the thoughts I think toward you, the thought of peace, and not of evil, to give you an expected end."* **(Jeremiah 29:11)**

God wants the best for his children just like a father wants his children to be successful and have a good life. On the other hand, Satan the devil plans to destroy the world with perversion, addictions, and wickedness into the world system.

The good news is, Jesus our Lord said, *"I have come to save the world and not to judge them"*. Anyone who knows their spiritual identity in Christ is not condemned. *"There is therefore now no condemnation to them which are in Christ Jesus, who walk not after the flesh, but after the spirit."(Roman 8:1) That means you should repent and change your way of life and stop pleasing your fleshly desires.*

I pray, May the power of the Holy Spirit free you from all forms of addictions and perversions, be free from condemnation in the name of mighty name of Jesus.

Apostle Paul said, *"If anyone is in Christ he or she is a new creature: old things have passed away; behold all things have become new."* **2 Corinthians 5:17**

Below is a testimony of a hopeless drug addict that proves how God deliver us from destruction.

"I was a chronic alcoholic, cocaine, crack, and a chain pot and cigarette smoker. I was hospitalized three times for alcohol

Introduction

overdose. I have been fighting this demon for several years. For eleven and a half months, I was living on the street. I had reached a breaking point when I was put out of the shelter and was robbed two times at gunpoint. I have nothing left than the cloth on my back, and I cry to God to help me. That was when God sent Pastor David from Jesus Witness Ministries to help me. I have been clean from drugs and alcohol addiction for more than three months. Presently, I am working, I have a roof over my head, and my wife is coming back to me." **(GS testifier)**

The testifier is one of my tenants now. To God be all the glory. The above testimony confirms that hope is not lost for anyone who has been a victim of all form of perversions, drugs, and alcohol. You can be free from the demonic slavery of perversions and addiction to drugs and alcohol. Knowing your spiritual identity in the Holy Spirit is the key. Holy Spirit is your helper, and one of his duties is to assist you to break free from the spirit of perversion and addictions. The good news is Jesus, and the Angels will be happy to bring you back home as God's children. I will be glad to join the Angels in Heaven who will be celebrating with you that you are free at last from demonic power of addiction and perversion. That will be your testimony in the mighty name of Jesus.

There is no other time in history where we have witnessed identity crisis than during this period. Satan and his demons have confused many people as regards their biological makeup and spiritual identity.

For example, imagine a man who after marrying a woman for twenty years with four children decided and declared that he is now a woman, *that he just discovered his true identity.*

The children are confused as to how many mothers they currently have. Also, a

Introduction

famous politician, who was married with children came out of the closet and declared that he was bi-sexual and his boyfriend was working for his government.

He is now a pastor in a gay church. ***If this is not an identity crisis, what is it?***

These are some of the examples of how Satan has succeeded in confusing the true identity of people as regards their biological makeup and sexual orientation.

Due to the lack of spiritual integrity which in turn leads to identity crisis makes people become the victim of perversions and addictions.

For example, when my job as an auditor moved me to the State of Florida in 2001, my landlady was *lesbian.* Her first question to me was, *"what do I think about gay people?"* I did not know her to be gay at that time. I responded by saying God opinion is more important than mine.

Know Your Spiritual Identity

I suggested we read what God says about gay-lesbian practices in **1 Corinthians 6:9-10**.

Apostle Paul Stated: "Do you not know that the unrighteous will not inherit the kingdom of God?

Do not be deceived. Neither fornicator, nor idolaters, nor adulterers, nor homosexuals, nor sodomites, nor thieves, nor covetous, nor drunkards, nor revilers, nor extortionist will inherit the kingdom of God **(I Corinthians 6:9-10).**

After reading the above Scriptures, I then asked, *'Is the Bible talking only about gay and Lesbian people?'* **She answered, "No!"**

I continued, 'As you can see both gay and straight people needed God's mercy and forgiveness. No one is better than the other because *all unrighteousness is a sin before*

Introduction

God.' She was comfortable to disclose to me her lesbian identity.

I learned that being *gay-lesbian* is not a choice. One of my questions to her was who played the role of a man in this kind of relationship? She answered by saying *"It does not matter; anyone can play the role of a man."*

I was thoroughly educated about the *gay-lesbian lifestyle*. After that, I have had *Gay and Lesbian* as tenants in my house. Also, I had had some gay students in my class when I was teaching at Newark Public School; these students will openly display their gay pride in the class.

Oftentimes, a side effect of pharmaceutical drugs is responsible for altering the hormones and genetic

Make-up of people. Some male are developing mammary organs like female and vice-visa. Regardless of your particular situation, God created you wonderfully as male or female. He can reverse any damage done to you by the devil.

A young boy was under the oppression of the evil spirit. It made him an autistics violent person. The School District classified him as special needs child and transferred him to a Handicap School.

The parent has to drive about one and half hours to get to that special school. The mother recognized that Jesus is using me as a vessel for healing and deliverance. She brought her son to me for deliverance.

After the deliverance prayers, Jesus revealed to me that the boy needs a name change before he could be delivered. I communicated the message to the parent. The parent took a step of faith and changed the boy's name.

Their faith draws power from Jesus and their son was delivered from the autistics

Introduction

behavior. The boy became a normal child and has returned to the regular high school in Maplewood School District.

To the Glory of God!

This testimony shows that *Jesus is still healing people today* from the oppression of the devil. If you are reading this book or you know anyone in similar situation your faith can draw power from Jesus and you shall be delivered.

The knowledge of knowing who you are in Christ Jesus will free you from the demonic powers.

You shall be delivered in the mighty name of Jesus. We should not be ignorant of satanic devices; therefore the following are some of the demonic vices that he has been using to put people in bondage morally and spiritually.

Know Your Spiritual Identity

MISSION

The mission of Jesus Witness Ministries is to utilize Bible knowledge to direct honest hearted people to Jesus, the only way, the truth, and life. Yes! Come to Jesus for salvation, for healing and deliverance (Matthew 11:28) (John 14:6. John 10:7-9 and Act 4:12).

Jesus said, "Jehovah's spirit is upon me, because he anointed me to declare good news to the poor, he sent me forth to preach a release to the captives and a recovery of sight to the blind, to send the crushed ones away with a release, and to preach Jehovah's acceptable year"(Luke 4:18).

We would not support false prophesy and Judgmental doctrines nor preach materialism as the only solution to people problems (Deuteronomy 18:20-22, Isaiah 65:13-16)

Mission

However, we would pray for Holy Spirit to give us the knowledge, the faith, resources and the power to accomplish the Lord's work(Matthew 6:33).

We would help the sheep-like one's to develop personal relationship with the Lord and to bear the fruitage of Gods' Holy Spirit in their daily lives-Galatians 5:22-24. We would recognize sins as spiritual sickness and would direct our members to be holy as God is holy with prayers and fasting (James 5: 13-16). We recognize Jesus position as an appointed judge of both the living and the dead.

Therefore, we would not engage in judgmental doctrines (John 5:22-24,30, Act 17:31, Matthew 7:1-5). We would encourage our members to develop their Gods' given talents and gifts to the maximum for the glory of our Lord through higher education and Bible studies.

Know Your Spiritual Identity

We would accept Tithes, Offering, First fruits, Seed of faith, Shiloh Sacrifice, Abel's Sacrifice, pledge and voluntary donations in cash, in services, in real property, plant and in Equipment to funds the global evangelism work of our LORD.

As the scripture says: "He who gives generously to the needy; his kindness lasts forever. "He that is showing favor to the lowly one is lending to Yahweh and his treatment He will repay to him."(2 Corinthians 9:6-9) (Malachi 3:10, Luke 6:38, Proverb 19:17).

We would devote of our resources to fund soul winning globally and to assist widows, orphans, and the poor in our midst (James 1:27, 1 Timothy 5:3-8, John 13:34-35).

CHAPTER 1
PERVERSIONS

Satan introduced perversion, such as bestiality and sodomy into the society to vandalize the handiwork of the God and depopulate the earth. He is determined to destroy God's creative work.

In some Countries of the world, some people are getting married to their pets, such as dogs, cow, reptiles and others animals.

For example, in Demark, there are some animal brothel that charges between $70 and $185 depending on the type of animal you choose as sex-partners.

In August, a woman in New Mexico tried to kill her roommates after they witnessed her having sex with a dog and admitting to having sex "multiple times" with the roommates' dogs.

Know Your Spiritual Identity

In September, a priest who was convicted of 24 counts of pedophilia in Canada had a bestiality record as well. These are a few examples of how Satan is busy using perversion to corrupt God's children. ***What are the health risks to those who practice bestiality because they did not know their spiritual identity in Christ Jesus?***

Any contact with the sexual organs of dogs, cattle, pigs, horses, and sheep can transmit leptospirosis bacterial disease to humans.

Leptospirosis can cause Meningitis which leads to death in about 10% of the cases. Echinococcosis is a parasitic worm from the feces of dogs, cats, and sheep can cause this disease.

The infections cause cysts in the lungs, liver, brain, spleen, heart, and kidneys. If not treated, this disease can be fatal.

Chapter 1 : Perversions

Rabies is a viral infection and one of the most severe of zoonoses, and rabies is transmitted from the saliva of cats, dogs, and horses. This viral infection does affect the central nervous system and is almost always fatal if not treated soon after the exposure.

Sexual contact with animals or SCA is also a risk factor for urological diseases among humans. In a study of 118 penile cancer patients, 44.9% patients had reported SCA leading to a conclusion that sex with animals is a risk factor for penile cancer and may be associated with venereal diseases.

Due to the high prevalence and associated risks for penile cancer and possibly sexually transmitted infections, the researchers felt that the issues of SCA merits close scientific attention.

Lastly, they suggested that initiatives to eradicate sex with animals should be considered. I agree with their concerns and suggestions for prevention of many possible diseases one can acquire due to SCA. In addition to the conditions one can catch through SCA, there is also the risk of injury that can be caused by large animals such as horses during the sexual intercourse.

For example, in 2005 a highly publicized case known as the "Enumclaw Horse Sex Case" became the landmark case to change the bestiality laws of the state of Washington where bestiality was legal since 1976.

A 45 years old aerospace engineer for Boeing died while receiving anal sex from a stallion which was videotaped by his friend. The story was reported in the Seattle Times.

The giant penis of the horse perforated his colon which led to his death. On February 11, 2006, due to the vast publicity of this case, the state of Washington outlawed bestiality and videotaping of any sexual contact with the dead or alive

Chapter 1 : Perversions

animals, making bestiality a Class C felony punishable by up to 15 years in prison.

According to the World Health Organization, although the zoo-noses represent significant public health risks, do not provide the needed steps to deal with this crime and downplay the seriousness of bestiality they are not prioritized by world health organization. Hundreds of thousands of people are dying by these diseases even though most of them can be prevented. Your loving God and father make his laws to protect you from diseases and from death.

CHAPTER 2

WHAT DOES BIBLE HISTORY SHOW?

In Noah's day immorality was the highest order of the day. The disobedient sons of God, look and saw the beautiful daughters of men. They came down from Heaven and started taken wives for themselves against God plan for their lives.

The sexual intercourse between the Angels and the daughter of men produced children. These (hybrid) children are called "giant" or men of renown.

The consequences of this disobedience were the Earth was polluted with crime and immorality. God was grieved in his hearts and regretted of creating men. God had no option than to destroy that world (Genesis

Chapter 2 : What Does Bible History Show?

6:2-7). The same wickedness was repeated in the days of Sodom and Gomorrah.

The sodomites will force innocent victims and strangers to have sex with them. The visiting Angels of God are not spared either, the Sodomites forced their way into Lot's house, who took the Angels in as a guest. The Bible reported that the men of Sodom were exceedingly wicked and sinful against the LORD (Genesis 13:13).

Jesus made references to the day of his second coming to the days of Noah.

In **Mathew 24:38-39,** Jesus said, *"For as in the days before the flood, they were eating and drinking, marrying and giving in marriage, until the day that Noah entered the ark, they did not know until the flood came and took them all away, so also will the coming of the Son of man be"*.

Before the flood, Noah was busy building an ark with faith. Then false prophets are mocking Noah for building an ark, saying, have you seen rain before? *Why are you building an ark?*

You must be going crazy. Similarly the false prophets and false Christ are busy preaching inclusiveness and material prosperity.

They have accepted immorality of same-sex marriages and bestiality in their churches. They have profaned the name of our God during such marriage between two females or between two men by blessing them in the name of God.

And some marry their pet in the church, just like in the day of Noah when the Angels are marrying the daughters of men.

No wonder, some children today cannot live a normal life but live like a beast, behave like an animal and they prey on innocent victims.

Chapter 2 : What Does Bible History Show?

Very shortly, what befell the wicked people of Sodom and Gomorrah and the ungodly men of Noah's day will soon befall this wicked generation.

CHAPTER 3
ILLICIT DRUGS AND ALCOHOL

Drugs are another weapon Satan is using to enslave the unsuspecting individual to destroy their mind and body, being God's temple. Your body is God's temple, and Satan wants to vandalize it and kills it so that it can't be useful to God. Recently, Nigeria government banned some drugs including Benadryl with codeine, tramadol, and Percocet to mention a few.

In other parts of the world the use of cocaine, cannabis, heroin, crack cocaine, and many other mind control drugs are on the rise.

Similarly, drug abuse in China became epidemic, facilitating the spread of HIV/AIDS. The Chinese government has made great efforts to address these problems,

Chapter 3: Illicit Drugs and Alcohol

focusing both on treatments of drug addiction and on harm-reduction programs.

The total economic cost of treating drugs and alcohol abusers in the United States of America was estimated at $246 billion in 1992. Alcohol abuse and alcoholism cost an estimated $148 billion, while drug abuse and drug dependence cost an estimated $98 billion.

The alcohol estimates for 1992 were similar to require estimates produced over the past 20 years when adjusted for inflation and population. In contrast, the drug estimates demonstrated a steady and robust pattern of increase.

More than $28 billion of the costs resulted from health care expenditures, which consisted of alcohol and drug abuse services and the costs of medical consequences of alcohol and drug abuse.

The more than $176 billion charges in productivity effects resulted from premature death, impaired productivity, institutionalized populations, incarceration, crime careers, and victims of alcohol-related crime and drug-related crime.

Other influences on society included crime, social welfare administration, motor vehicle crashes, and fire destruction and cost more than $40 billion. The government, private insurance, and victims bore most of the economic burden of alcohol and drug problems. Alcohol abusers and their households bore $66.8 billion of the alcohol-related costs; drug abusers and their families bore $42.9 billion of the drug-related charges.

The economic effects of alcohol and drug abuse have increased an estimated 12.5 percent between 1992 and 1995 due to inflation and growth in the population.

Chapter 3 : Illicit Drugs and Alcohol

These are the weapon of oppression and depression the devil is using to destroy people destiny and to confuse them of their spiritual identity.

CHAPTER 4

PERSECUTION OF GOD'S CHILDREN

Satan and his agents are killing millions of believers for upholding faith in Jesus Christ. And if your faith is different from the religion of the fanatics you're at risk. Christians the world over have been persecuted and some are being beheaded by Islamic terrorist group in many countries.

For example in Afghanistan, Arabian countries, and particularly in Nigeria, the Boko-haram (which means western education is sin) terrorist group started by bombing Churches and killing Christians in their effort to Islamized Nigeria. In 2015 they kidnapped 300 Chibork school girls, and in 2017 another 115 Depeche schoolgirls were abducted.

Chapter 4 : Persecution of God's Children

Another example was the Assembly Bill 2943 in California banning the sale of any book (Bible, Quran or Deliverance Book) that speaks against homosexuality. Any effort to liberate people who have been a victim of perversion is declared illegal.

Banning the Bible and the Christian texts was an attack on Christian's faith. Bill 2943 will open the door to persecute the believers who uphold God's standard on morality. Some ritualists will demand fresh human body parts to make money. Some cultist and street gangs demand that sleeping with minor children and the drinking of human blood is required for initiation of a new member.

The Bible says, *"Woe unto them that call evil good, and good evil; that put darkness for light, and light for darkness; that put bitter for sweet, and sweet for bitter! Woe unto them that are wise in their own eyes, and prudent in their sight!"* **(Isaiah 5:20-21)**

CHAPTER 5

FALSE RELIGION

The Bible helps us to know that Satan will keep transforming himself into an Angel of light. Jesus predicted this when he says, "there will be false prophets and false teachers and false Apostles representing the devil, but by their fruits, you shall know them.

If anyone claims to be a man of God and prophesy and the prediction did not come true, the prophesy is not from God but the devil and do not be afraid of him the Bible says.

For example, in Nigeria, every available kiosk, shops, flats, and abandoned factories have been converted to religion houses. The teaching is either materialism or miracles, yet ritual killings, official corruptions,

Chapter 5 : False Religion

kidnapping, armed robbery and witchcraft practices are on the increase.

Religion did not produce God-fearing people but ungodly men and women. Many false prophets has been prophesying falsehood and it is common to hear this false teachers asking their victim to pay large sum of money so that they can go to heaven or to become rich.

The Bible says, those who are determined to be rich shall fall into temptation and a hurtful desires; the love of money is the root of all evils. Other false religion popularly known as Jehovah's Witnesses engaged in predicting the end of the world in 1914, 1919, 1935 and 1975 and in 1985 but all their false prophesy fell to the ground. God did not send them. They are inspired by the devil. This cult religion employed social killing (Shunning policy). They uses FEAR of shunning to separate families in their effort to keep their members in bondage. They shared common methodology with Book-Haram. They forbid higher education for their members to prevent them from having critical thinking skills. To enforce shunning policy and hatred, they misapplied Jesus word in Matthew 10:37: *"He who loves his father or mother more than me is not worthy of me. Also he who loves his son or daughter more than me is not worthy of me"*.

These false teachers have ruined many families by misapplying the above scriptures by replacing Jesus with the 'Watchtower Society. That means Jehovah is synonymous with Watchtower Society.

Their false teachings have ruined many homes. The fear of shunning kept many people in this false religion. For example, I knew that the Watchtower Society was a false prophet after failed prophesy about the end of the world in 1975.

Chapter 5 : False Religion

I have no courage to leave due to fear of shunning. Fear kept me there for another thirty years until Jesus delivered me from them. The Bible says,

For such are false apostles, deceitful workers, transforming themse*lves into the apostles of Christ and no marvel; for Satan himself is transformed into an angel of light. Therefore it is* no great thing if his ministers also be transformed as the ministers of righteousness; *whose end shall be according to their works.* **(2 Corinthian 11:13-15)**

God said……,

"When a prophet speaketh in the name of the LORD, if the thing follow not, nor come to pass, that is the thing which the LORD hath not spoken, *but* the prophet hath spoken it presumptuously: thou shalt not be afraid of him" **(Dueteronomy 18:22) (Mark 13:22 2Timothy 4:3, 2 John 1:9-11).**

When Boko-Haram Terrorist group are killing people physically and forbidding western education, the Watchtower Society are killing people socially and forbidding higher education for their members.

At this time of the end the rise of false prophets and false Christ will abound. They will show signs and wonders and mislead many with their false teachings. *"Heaven and Earth shall pass away but my word shall not pass away"*, Jesus said. You can see why endurance is needed to be saved.

CHAPTER 6
ENDURANCE IS REQUIRED FOR SALVATION

Materialism and immorality have taken over the churches and the false prophets are busy diverting the attention of the people to the glamour of materialism and adopting immorality as alternative life-style.

There is no doubt people are suffering from economic problems, marital issues, generational curses, health issues, the problem of barrenness, and persecution of God's people.

Due to these problems people are going from one church to another looking for solutions and miracles to solve their problems. It is sad to say that solution is not in churches nor is it with the witch doctors.

Jesus is the answers to all problems. He offered two solutions to all these problems.

One solution is found in Matthew 6:24-33 where Jesus said:

"No one can serve two masters; for either he will hate the one and love the other, or else he will be loyal to the one and despise the other. You cannot serve God and mammon. "Therefore I say to you, do not worry about your life, what you will eat or what you will drink; nor about your body, what you will put on. Is not life more than food and the body more than clothing? Look at the birds of the air, for they neither sow nor reap nor gather into barns; yet your heavenly Father feeds them. Are you not of more value than they?

Which of you by worrying can add one cubit to his stature? So why do you worry about clothing? Consider the lilies of the field, how they grow: they neither toil nor

Chapter 6 : Endurance is Required for Salvation

spin; and yet I say to you that even Solomon in all his glory was not arrayed like one of these. Now if God so clothes the grass of the field, which today is, and tomorrow is thrown into the oven, will He not much more clothe you, O you of little faith? Therefore do not worry, saying, 'What shall we eat?' or 'What shall we drink?' or 'What shall we wear?' For after all these things the Gentiles seek. For your heavenly Father knows that you need all these things. But seek first the kingdom of God and His righteousness, and all these things shall be added to you.

Number one solution to life economic problems is to seek God first, create a job with your talent and live as holy as possible, then all the problems you may face will be over because God will supply all that you need to survive each day of the week.

If God supplies over three million Jews with provision in the wilderness for forty years, He will supply all your needs until Jesus comes.

Jesus reveals the second solution to me when I had personal encounter with Him on July 2, 2018, I was in a dream of the night, when Jesus told me to open my Bible, which was under my pillow to the book of Mark 13:13. I woke up and immediately open my Bible to Mark 13:13 as instructed. *It reads, "And you shall be hated of all men for my name's sake: but he that shall ENDURE to the end shall be saved".*

As I was meditating over the meaning of this Scripture and what shall I do with this information, I noticed the word Endurance stood out as a condition for salvation.

The word endurance is one of the fruits of God's Holy Spirit. The word endurance means to suffer-for a long time. I said to my Lord, this is not a good news message.

Chapter 6 : Endurance is Required for Salvation

Endure suffering for a long time is not one of the regular prayer points. At this time of the end, no Christian prays to suffer at all, talk less of suffering for a long time. All our prayers points are to move us from glory to glory.

Endurance is not needed when one is living a prosperous life. Endurance is not needed when one is enjoying good quality of life. Endurance is not needed when one is living in abundance.

Why should a Christian be ready to suffer for a long time or need endurance in other to be saved? Jesus answered this question: You shall be hated of all men for my name's sake.

That a slave is not greater than his master, if the world hates me, then Christ followers should expect the same hatred from the world. Christians need endurance at this time of the end more than any other time in history.

Jesus further said, there will be great affliction, such as was not from the beginning of creation unto this time, neither shall it be.

The rise of false prophets and false Christs will abound. They will show signs and wonders and mislead many with their false teachings. *"Heaven and Earth shall pass away but my word shall not pass away",* Jesus said. You can see why endurance is needed to be saved.

What should Christians do?

Jesus again answered this question: Watch and Pray. ***What does it means to watch?*** Is it to form a Vigilante Group in every villages, hamlets, towns and Cities? Is it to ban Muslim from entering our Countries? The answer is no.

Chapter 6 : Endurance is Required for Salvation

The improved security and vigilante group will not stop the hatred and the killing of Christians. Christian must watch for signs and physical manifestation of Jesus words and the signs of his second coming. They must come to pass.

Prophesies about the persecution and the killing of Christians must come to pass in other to know genuine Christians from fake Christians. Jesus reveals to Apostle John in Revelation 20:4 that he saw thrones and people that sat on them, he also saw the souls of them that were beheaded for witnessing to Jesus, and for the word of God, and those who had not worshipped the beast, neither his image, neither had received his mark upon their foreheads, or in their hands; and that and they lived and reigned with Christ a thousand years.

Therefore if you have seeing Christians being beheaded in Syria, Afghanistan, Iraq,

Saudi Arabia or in Nigeria, it is in fulfillment of Jesus prophesies in Revelation 20:4.

True Christians need to pray for the spirit of endurance because your faith will be tested beyond human capacity.

For example, four armed men entered into a mega Church and fire into the ceiling. They shouted, "if you are ready to die for Jesus move to the right.

If you want to deny Jesus and live, you can go. Ninety five percent of the church members denied Jesus and left the church. Then the armed men removed their face-mask and said to the people on the right, we are not here to kill you but want to know who are genuine Christians; now let the service continue", they said.

From the above experience, we can see that God is looking for those who will pass the test of faith and endure to the end to inherit God's Kingdom.

Chapter 6 : Endurance is Required for Salvation

The persecution and the killing of Christians allow Jesus to identify those who truly love him and those who deserve to be in God's Kingdom. One may asked, why would a loving God allow the persecution of his servants? Another illustration that comes to mind to answer this question is precious metals like Gold or Diamond.

It must pass through the fire and be purified before they can be useful. Similarly true Christian must pass through the test of their faith, it is like passing through the fire, and passing through the flood and other form of purification before one can qualify to rule with Jesus.

For example, since February 19, 2018 one the kidnapped Dapchi School girls, Leah Sharibu, a Christian was still in bondage of Boko Haram Terrorist group because of her faith in Jesus.

Know Your Spiritual Identity

It calls for wisdom, then, to be spiritually awake to watch for the signs of Jesus second coming as foretold in Mark 13 and Mathew 24.

The second advice of Jesus was to pray. What shall Christians be praying for? Shall we pray for fire to come down from Heavens to consume our persecutors and killers? Or should we pray for endurance to be able to pass the test of our love and faith in Jesus? Or should we be praying that our flight should not be during the winter? *Jesus said, when they persecute you in one city flee to another city and before you flee to all the city, the son of man will come* (Mathew 10:23).

Remember the word of our Lord when he said, **"A servant is not greater than his master; If they persecuted me, they will also persecute you"** (John 15:20).

Chapter 6 : Endurance is Required for Salvation

All true Christians should be prepared to endure persecution, and all kinds of evil against you for Christ's name sake. Jesus said a time is coming when people will put you out of their synagogues, and whoever that kill you will think that he does God service. (John 16:2)

In fulfillment of the above Scriptures, the fanatical religionist are practicing shunning and killing of anyone or any member who did not believe in their false doctrine. These fanatics will praise God after beheading people with the hope that, the act of committing murder will qualify them to make heavens and one thousand virgins.

In all these endurance is required to maintain our love and faith for the king of kings, Jesus Christ. He who loves his life will lose it, and he that loses his life for my sake will find it, Jesus assure Christians.

Therefore we should pray without ceasing for the spirit of endurance. We should pray for the fruits of endurance. We should pray for more faith and unconditional love for our God. Even if our lives are lost, it will be temporary because Jesus promised the resurrection of the faithful to reward them with everlasting life.

One of the outstanding servants of God who endured severe persecution was Apostle Paul, he wrote about the assurance of the resurrection hope,

"For we know that if our earthly house, this tent, *is destroyed, we have a building from God, a house not made with hands, eternal in the heavens. For in this we groan, earnestly desiring to be clothed with our habitation which is from heaven, if indeed, having been clothed, we shall not be found naked. For we who are in this* tent groan, being burdened, not because we want to be

Chapter 6 : Endurance is Required for Salvation

unclothed, but further clothed, that mortality may be swallowed up by life.

Now He who has prepared us for this very thing is God, who also has given us the Spirit as guarantee. *So we are* always confident, knowing that while we are at home in the body we are absent from the Lord. *for we walk by faith, not by sight. We are confident, yes, well pleased rather to be absent from the body and to be present with the Lord"* **(2 Corinthians 5:1-8).**

All Christian should have the same mental attitude like Apostle Paul in the above example. We should count it a privilege to give up our lives for Jesus Christ who paid a supreme sacrifice to purchase us from the bondage of sin and death.

"If anyone wants to be my disciple, let him carry his torture stake (cross) and follow me.

Know Your Spiritual Identity

What happens to Jesus disciples after he went back to heavens?

Did Jesus words and prophesies about those who want to be his followers come to pass and how do they die? Did Jesus prophesies come to pass about the nature of their death? You can be sure that any educated, first-century Roman citizen would have laughed at any prediction that within three centuries the Christian faith would be the official faith of the empire.

But Jesus formed his disciples into the backbone of the church and gave them the most extraordinary task imaginable: calling the entire world, including the mightiest empire ever known, to repentance and faith in the risen Christ.

Persecution of early Christians:

Many wonders how the 12 apostles died, but The New Testament tells of the

Chapter 6 : Endurance is Required for Salvation

fate of only two of the apostles: Judas, who betrayed Jesus and then went out and hanged himself, and James the son of Zebedee, who was executed by Herod about 44 AD (Acts 12:1-2). Read how each of the apostles spread out to minister and evangelize and how many of the apostles died for their faith.

They suffered greatly for their faith and in most cases met violent deaths on account of their bold witness.

For example, Peter and Paul both martyred in Rome about 66 AD, during the persecution under Emperor Nero. Paul was beheaded. Peter was crucified, upside down at his request, since he did not feel he was worthy to die in the same manner as his Lord.

Andrew went to the "land of the man-eaters," in what is now the Soviet Union. Christians there claim him as the first to bring the gospel to their land.

He also preached in Asia Minor, modern-day Turkey, and in Greece, where he is said to have been crucified.

Thomas was probably most active in the area east of Syria. Tradition has him preaching as far east as India, where the ancient Marthoma Christians revere him as their founder.

They claim that he died there when pierced through with the spears of four soldiers. Philip possibly had a powerful ministry in Carthage in North Africa and then in Asia Minor, where he converted the wife of a Roman proconsul. In retaliation the proconsul had Philip arrested and cruelly put to death.

Matthew the tax collector and writer of a Gospel, ministered in Persia and Ethiopia. Some of the oldest reports say he was not martyred, while others say he was stabbed to death in Ethiopia.

Chapter 6 : Endurance is Required for Salvation

Bartholomew had widespread missionary travels attributed to him by tradition: to India with Thomas, back to Armenia, and also to Ethiopia and Southern Arabia. There are various accounts of how he met his death as a martyr for the gospel.

James the son of Alpheus, is one of at least three James referred to in the New Testament. There is some confusion as to which is which, but this James is reckoned to have ministered in Syria.

The Jewish historian Josephus reported that he was stoned and then clubbed to death.

Simon the Zealot so the story goes, ministered in Persia and was killed after refusing to sacrifice to the sun god.

Matthias was the apostle chosen to replace Judas. Tradition sends him to Syria with Andrew and to death by burning.

John is the only one of the company generally thought to have died a natural death from old age. He was the leader of the church in the Ephesus area and is said to have taken care of Mary the mother of Jesus in his home. During Domitian's persecution in the middle 90's, he was exiled to the island of Patmos.

There he is credited with writing the last book of the New Testament--the Revelation. An early Latin tradition has him escaping unhurt after being cast into boiling oil at Rome.

The above examples of how early Christian made supreme sacrifice for their faith is not to scare you as a believer but to prepare your mind like a soldier who enroll to serve his country knowing that the chances of losing his or her life is real for fighting for his/her country.

Chapter 6 : Endurance is Required for Salvation

Persecution of Christian Today

Similarly modern day Christian are not immune to persecution and painful death for ones faith in Christ.

Presently many people are being killed for their faith in Christ Jesus in fulfilment of Revelation 20:4.

For example, since February 19, 2018 one the kidnapped Dapchi School girls, Leah Sharibu, a Christian was still in bondage of Boko Haram Terrorist group because of her faith in Jesus.

The news of her death was rude awakening to the authority however government and the journalist call it a fake news.

When I was about to pray to God for vengeance against the persecutors of Christians, Jesus corrected me and re-directed me to pray for the spirit of endurance instead.

He said, *"Those who endure to the end shall be saved."* A slave is not greater than his master. If they persecuted him and kill him, his disciples should expect the same treatment". *He that endures to the end shall be saved, Jesus says"* (**Mark 13:13 and Mathew 24:13**).

If the men and women who serve their nation in the military are willing to lay down their lives in defense of the country, all Christians should be able to endure all form of persecution to the end of our mortal life. Christian should not be afraid of those that can kill the body but cannot kill the soul. May Jesus grant us the spirit of endurance to the end of our live? Amen

CHAPTER 7

GROSS DARKNESS COVERED THE PEOPLE:

God reveals to me that darkness has covered the world and gross darkness the people and they are in the dark because they did not have the light of God and they are subject to manipulation and confusion.

They are the victim of an identity crisis foisted on them by Satan, the devil. This identity crisis is pervasive in our society; it cuts across social, religion and economic status. Some famous politicians, and women, young people and adults have all become the victim of an identity crisis.

Today some gay men or Lesbians are pastors of Churches. In the United States of America and in India, same sex marriages are legal.

The same-sex will marry each other, and some cases adopt their own children. The United States laws protect this life-style. It is called human rights. There is no reason why anyone should be gay phobia or be paranoid and be fearful of people with different sexual orientation. Instead, one should have compassion and pray for the people who have been a victim of an identity crisis. Satan has confused people as to their own biological identity and spiritual identity.

As we are very close to the end of this wicked system, the god of this world (Satan) is desperate, confusing unsuspecting individual as to their own biological identity and spiritual identity. **(Isaiah 60:1-2)**

The Apostle Paul was alluding to this when he wrote, "But even if our gospel is veiled, it is veiled to those who are perishing, whose minds the god of this age has blinded, who do not believe, lest the light of the gospel of the glory of Christ,

Chapter 7 : Gross Darkness Covered the People:

who is the image of God, should shine on them."

This confusion has gone beyond religion, politics, and academics. Satan has a master plan to depopulate the world, to confuse the world and to fight God's children. Satan is using perversion, drugs and alcohol addiction to enslave the people. Also, he is unleashing persecution on God's children.

Jesus predicted this when he said, "Then they will deliver you up to tribulation and kill you, and all nations will hate you for my name's sake, and those who endure to the end, shall be saved".

These are some of the composite signs of the end times." (Matthew 24:9-14, 2 Corinthians 4:3-4)

On June 26, 2015, the United States Supreme Court granted same-sex partners the same rights and privileges like a straight couple. "Obergefell v. Hodges, U.S. (2015) is a landmark civil rights case in which the Supreme Court of the United States ruled that the fundamental right to marry be guaranteed to same-sex couples by both the Due Process Clause and the Equal Protection Clause of the Fourteenth Amendment to the United States Constitution.

The 5–4 ruling requires all fifty states to perform and recognize the marriages of same-sex couples on the same terms and conditions as the marriages of opposite-sex couples, with all the accompanying rights and responsibilities".

Discrimination in marriage is against the law of the land. The gay and lesbians have equal rights before the judge to marry whomever they desire. That shows that Satan has succeeded in confusing the highest court in the land to rule against God's laws that forbid the practice of same-sex marriages.

Chapter 7 : Gross Darkness Covered the People:

The New York Times, September 1, 2015, reported about a Christian official, Ms. Kim Davis who has refused to issue marriage licenses to same-sex couples in Kentucky despite the U.S. Supreme Court orders. She said, "Her action was under God's authority." She is a modern-day example of three Hebrews boys namely, Shadrach, Meshach and Abednego who refused to worship the image of King Nebuchadnezzar. The same episode is playing out in our modern time.

Kim Davis has the right to obey God who said, *"You shall not lie with a male as with a woman. It is an abomination. Nor shall you mate with any animal, to defile yourself with it. Nor shall any woman stand before an animal to mate with it. It is a perversion."*

Also, "Whoever lies with an animal shall surely be put to death."**(Leviticus 18:22-23, Exodus 22:19).**

Know Your Spiritual Identity

Many believers will go to jail, and some will be killed. This is a time of testing to identify the true sons of God from false prophets. The true believers will rather pay with their lives than to compromise their faith in God.

CHAPTER 8

YOU SHALL REAP WHAT YOU SOW

What are the consequences of same-sex behavior?

The World Health Organization's Guidelines for the Management of Sexually Transmitted Infections was published in 2004, sexually transmitted disease (STD) rates among men who have sex with men (MSM) have continued to increase across the United States and abroad. Factors associated with increased rates of STDs include the loss of fear regarding human immunodeficiency virus (HIV) transmission because of the increased manageability of the infection, the use of the Internet as an efficient way to find sex partners, increasing use of erectile dysfunction agents, and possibly the expanding role of oral sex in STD transmission.

In many settings, the increases in STDs have been associated with increases in HIV, but not invariably, suggesting the possibility that "serosorting" (choosing HIV-seroconcordant partners) or other harm-reduction strategies and the differential prevalence of specific STDs in different subpopulations of MSM may lead to differential infection transmission. Although many of the new infections are occurring among younger MSM, a substantial burden of HIV and STD morbidity continues to be found among middle-aged and older men as well.

One of the significant factors facilitating the increased risk-taking behavior by MSM is the use of dis-inhibiting substances, including alcohol, crystal methamphetamine, and other recreational drugs.

Chapter 8 : You Shall Reap What You Sow

Prevention interventions should focus on the specific situations in which these substances are used, given that the aggregate amount of substance use is generally not the primary predictor of risk-taking behavior; acquisition of HIV and other STDs is more directly related to the use of these substances in conjunction with unprotected sex. Among the drugs most highly associated with risk-taking behavior are methamphetamines and erectile dysfunction drugs.

"Although a preponderance of the literature regarding MSM and STD/HIV risk and prevalence is from the industrialized world. Recent data suggest that HIV and STD prevalence and incidence are also significant in the developing world, with rates of syphilis, gonorrhea, and Chlamydia in MSM cohorts in Africa, Latin America, and Asia greatly exceeding those of the general population in each of those settings".

Know Your Spiritual Identity

The consequences of heavy drinking called alcoholics. Diseases of alcoholics include Liver disease, Pancreatitis, Cancer, Ulcers and gastrointestinal problems, Immune system dysfunction, brain damage, Osteoporosis, Heart disease, and accidents and injuries.

The Bible says those who know their God shall be active and carry out great exploits. That means if you know your spiritual identity in Jesus, you shall be healthy and you shall be wealthy too. **(Daniel 11:32)**

The Bible says, "Do not be deceived, God is not mocked; for whatever a man sows, that he will also reap. For he who sows to his flesh will of the flesh reap corruption, but he who sows to the Spirit will of the Spirit reap everlasting life **(Galatia 6:7-8)**

CHAPTER 9

GOD OF MERCY AND DISCIPLINE

On September 1, 2015, Mrs. Kim Davis was jailed for obeying God and for disobeying the United States Supreme Court orders to issue marriage licenses for same-sex couples.

My hearts was grieved. I asked God a specific question about what he would do in the case of believers like Mrs. Kim Davis who will rather pay with their lives rather than to disobey him?

I then reminded him of how he saved the lives of Shadrack and Abednego who were thrown into the fiery furnace when King Nebuchadnezzar passed a similar law requiring all citizens to worship his idol.

Know Your Spiritual Identity

It is the law of the land that all citizens should worship the image of the king with the capital punishment of the fiery furnace. (Daniel 3:1-30) *Similarly, it is the law of the Supreme Court of the United States to legalize same-sex couples as husband and wife, regardless of God's laws* in Leviticus 18:22-23.

On September 4, 2015, God answered my prayers and Kim Davis was released. God told me to read his plan in the book of Isaiah 42:8-18.

Which read, "I am the Lord, that is my name, and my glory I will not give to another, Nor My praise to carved images. Behold, the former things have come to pass, and new things I declare; before they spring forth I tell you of them."

"Sing to the Lord a new song, And His praise from the ends of the earth, You who go down to the sea, and all that is in it, You

Chapter 9 : God of Mercy and Discipline

coastlands and you inhabitants of them! Let the wilderness and its cities lift up their voice, the villages that Kedar inhabits. Let the inhabitants of Sela sing, Let them shout from the top of the mountains".

"Let them give glory to the Lord, and declare His praise in the coastlands. The Lord shall go forth like a mighty man; He shall stir up His zeal like a man of war. He shall cry out, yes, shout aloud; He shall prevail against His enemies. I have held my peace a long time, I have been still and restrained Myself. Now I will cry like a woman in labor, and I will pant and gasp at once. I will lay waste the mountains and hills, And dry up all their vegetation; I will make the rivers coastlands, And I will dry up the pools".

"I will bring the blind by a way they did not know; I will lead them in paths they have not known. I will make darkness light before them, and crooked places straight. These

things I will do for them, and not forsake them. They shall be turned back, they shall be much ashamed, who trust in carved images, who say to the molded images, 'You are our gods.'" "Hear you deaf; and look, you blind, that you may see

I did not understand the above meaning of what God is saying to me here. However, I prayed to the Holy Spirit to help me to understand what God is saying in these scriptures.

God disclosed to me that he would show compassion and mercy to those who are confused by Satan because they are the victims of identity crisis and perversion. As regards any country that contravened his laws, God says he will discipline them for passing laws that contradict his laws and principles.

He said, my assignment is to remain faithful and to praise his holy name. That

Chapter 9 : God of Mercy and Discipline

encounter changed my perspective on how to interact with people who are the victim of Satan confusion.

They are undergoing a spiritual identity crisis. Presently, there is legislation in the state of Californian to ban the sale of the Bible because it forbids the practice of sodomy. (Leviticus 18:22-29). Satan will not rest in fighting God's children.

CHAPTER 10

THE SOLUTIONS TO IDENTITY CRISIS

What are the solutions to this identity crisis? God's Knowledge is power to freedom from the vices of the devil.

Your identity in Christ is a sure way to your liberations. Jesus had conquered Satan in Heaven, and he will soon be defeated here on earth. Very soon, all men and women will be free from Satan domination and confusion.

Remember your fight is not against flesh and blood. *The Bibles say, "For we do not wrestle against flesh and blood, but against principalities, against powers, against the rulers of the darkness of this age, against spiritual hosts of wickedness in the heavenly places."* **(Ephesians 6:10-15)**

Chapter 10 : The Solutions to Identity Crisis

Since no flesh and blood can fight against the rulers of darkness, one will need the assistance of Jesus Christ and his military commander, Michael the archangel to destroy the work of the enemy in your life.

Jesus will disarm the principalities and powers; he has made a public spectacle of them, triumphing over them in it." **(Colossians 2:15; Revelation 12:7-12)**

Regardless of the satanic method of persecution and perversion, you can be more than Conquerors if you have the light and know your spiritual identity. We have the assurance of victory against the enemy.

We should remember the Apostle Paul statement when he said, *"For though we walk in the flesh, we do not war according to the flesh. For the weapons of our warfare are not carnal but mighty in God for pulling down strongholds, casting down arguments*

Know Your Spiritual Identity

and every high thing that exalts itself against the knowledge of God, bringing every thought into captivity to the obedience of Christ." **(2 Corinthian 10:3-5)**

All believers should not rest both in prayer and fasting and for God to grant us the spirit of endurance and victory over the evil. We are very close to the final day of this wicked generation. Satan knows his time is up. Another example was my conversations with a young man I met in my evangelizing work. He had decided to commit suicide.

He boasted of His criminal exploits by saying, and I quote, "I have nothing left to do because I had committed all the crime in the world, such as three murders, rapes, robberies, drugs and alcohol." *What else can I live for Pastor he asked?*

He decided to commit suicide because he had finished with all the possible crime.

Chapter 10 : The Solutions to Identity Crisis

Then I told him there are many things he has not done. What is it, he asked? I said, you still need to give your life to Christ and become a prophet of God. He asked, "do you think that God can forgive me? I said, YES. We are all under the grace of redemption (Ephesians 2:7-8; John 1:17).

Apostle Paul said, *"There is therefore now no condemnation to those who are in Christ Jesus, who do not walk according to the flesh, but according to the Spirit. For the law of the Spirit of life in Christ Jesus has made me free from the law of sin and death."* **(Romans 8:1-2).**

The result was that this man has changed and has overcome his drugs addictions. All glory is to Jesus and my father in the Heavens. Developing relationships with God is very crucial in living a life of Christ. This book will assist people to identify your true identity in Christ Jesus and to find solutions to your identity crisis.

Know Your Spiritual Identity

God, Jesus, and the Holy Spirit require his adopted children and believers to have a form of spiritual identification to gain access to his throne of grace. *What do I mean?*

Many people don't have relationship with God, nor with Jesus, and have interaction with Holy Spirit. The first step is to know yourself.

If you don't know who you are spiritually, Satan and his agents will confuse you biologically and spiritually. Not until you solve this "Spiritual Identity Crisis", you would not be able to have access to your inheritance as God's children. Knowing your Christian identity will enable you to defend your faith and fulfill your destiny. Your behavior is motivated by what you believe.

Once you embrace your true identity in Christ by trusting what Jesus did for you, and whom God says you are and how the Holy Spirit view you personally, your

Chapter 10 : The Solutions to Identity Crisis

behavior will begin to reflect your new identity.

Why is it important to find a solution to your spiritual identity?

CHAPTER 11

THE IMPORTANCE OF FINDING ONE'S IDENTITY

The illustration of a young man will help you to know how important it is to find a solution to one identity crisis.

The name is Daniel Klein (not the real name). Daniel Klein was growing up without a father figure in his life. He struggled all his life without knowing his father.

One day he summons the courage to ask his mother, who is my father? The mother told him the story of how he was born and that his father was a president of a powerful country, with several billions of investments all over the world. She further showed him the picture of his father on the pages of the newspaper.

Chapter 11: The Importance of Finding One's Identity

At hearing this story that he has a rich and powerful father, he was elated, and he has the hope of becoming rich and becoming powerful man like his father. He did not stop there, and he started comparing his face and physical features of his father to himself.

He started reading more about his father. He began writing a letter to his father and calling press conferences to get the attention of his father.

He has tried many times to get his father attention and recognition but to no avail. Why did Daniel Klein not give up in search of his biological father and to have a relationship with him? He knows that the very day his father accepted him as his son, his economic worries are over.

The son can now claim his right as a son. He will become an influential person like his father. He will be surrounded by the rich and famous.

Know Your Spiritual Identity

Unfortunately, his father is fearful of his political career. He denied fatherhood to his son. Daniel Klein is still begging to have a relationship with his father. Unlike Daniel Klein's father, the believers have a powerful father in the Heavens, and he owns all the riches and glory of this world.

Finding who He is and what you can do to have a personal relationship with him is a must, if you want to overcome the vices of the devil and if you want to become rich and famous.

The good news is, your heavenly father is not afraid of men, and he wants to welcome you back home, like a prodigal son's father. God will hold a party with the Angels in Heaven and rejoice over you, if you repent and free from drugs and alcohol and all the vices of the devil.

Your Heavenly father said, *if your sin is red like red ink, he will make it white like*

Chapter 11: The Importance of Finding One's Identity

snow, in another word, your God and father can supernaturally change your present situation to a better condition.

There is nothing impossible for God to do. If you have made a wrong choice in life, don't give up, God is waiting for you to start a relationship with you through Jesus our Lord and Savior. (Isaiah 1:18)

Finding a solution to your spiritual identity crisis will change your life forever. In our illustration above, Daniel Klein will not give up until he establishes a personal relationship with his father who has limited power and resources to help him.

On the other hands your Heavenly father has unlimited power and resources to support his earthly children.

Don't give up!!

You shall dominate sickness in the mighty name of Jesus. You shall overcome perversion in your life in the mighty name of Jesus. You shall not lack any good things in the mighty name of Jesus.

You shall discover your destiny in the might name of Jesus. Unlike Daniel Klein, your father will not reject you in the mighty name of Jesus.

After you have developed a personal relationship with your father and find solutions to your spiritual identity crisis, you can now determine like Apostle Paul who said, *"Who shall separate us from the love of Christ? Shall tribulation, distress, persecution, famine, nakedness, peril, or sword? In all these things we are more than conquerors through Him who loved us. For I am persuaded that neither death nor life, nor angels nor principalities nor powers, nor things present nor things to come, nor height nor depth, nor any other created thing, shall be able to separate us from the*

Chapter 11: The Importance of Finding One's Identity

love of God which is in Christ Jesus our Lord". **(Romans 8:35, 37-39)**

Yes, you will have the power to overcome any form of perversion, addiction, and criminality in your bloodline.

CHAPTER 12

THE IDENTITY KEYS THAT BREAK ALL BARRIERS

The knowledge of your new spiritual identity can break all yoke in your lives. The anointing of God in your life shall break all the barriers in your lives in the mighty name of Jesus.

The third question is what is my identity with Jesus and how is my relationship with Jesus? Who am I according to Christ Jesus? The good news is Jesus has come to save sinners, and He did not come to condemn sinners.

The following are the spiritual identity in God the father, God the Son and God the Holy Spirit that will liberate you from any form of demonic vices. For examples, "the very day I know my spiritual identity, my life changed forever.

Chapter 12: The Identity Keys That Break all Barriers

I stop all the works of the flesh, and I started to bear the fruits of God's Holy Spirit in my life, "the writer says." Some People recognized this and started to call me Pastor. You too can have a good name and title if you know who you are in Christ.

Jesus has given you the power and the keys to bind and to lose and to overcome spiritual challenges' in perversion and addiction. I have assembled 25 spiritual keys of identity in God the father, in Jesus, and in the Holy Spirit. **(Mathew 18:18)**

The first step in finding the solution to a spiritual identity crisis is to know who you are. You will do well to ask the following questions.

Who am I? Why am I here? What is my destiny? **What is my relationship with God the father?**

What is my relationship with Jesus Christ?

Know Your Spiritual Identity

What is my relationship with God's Holy Spirit?

Before you answer the above questions, you need to know who you are as a person. *What is your biological makeup, your physical and spiritual make-up?* I am happy to inform you that you're a spirit being that has a soul. You lived in a material body (dust).

Spiritual Identity Key1

You are a SPIRIT, You have a SOUL, and you live in a BODY. You are *a spirit being* because your Heavenly *Father is spirit* and created you in *his image as a spirit person.*

You have a soul that communicates messages between *your spirit* and *your body*. Just like the battery in your car transmit information between the engine and the body mechanics.

Chapter 12: The Identity Keys That Break all Barriers

Your body is made of dust and enjoys sinning and worldly things like perversion, drugs, and alcohol. Apostle Paul stated, *"Now may the God of peace Himself sanctify you completely; and may your whole spirit, soul, and body be preserved blameless at the coming of our Lord Jesus Christ."* (I Thessalonians 5:23).

If you know your spiritual identity as spirit and that you were created in God's image, you will preserved your whole spirit, soul and body as holy as possible. You will run away from any sin that can destroy your life.

This knowledge will enable you to know God's purpose and plan for your lives and how to fulfill your destiny. One of God's plans for your life is to make you wealthy and to make you healthy so that you can reflect his glory. **(3 John 2:1)**

Know Your Spiritual Identity

Spiritual Identity Key 2

'You are "gods" *"you are all sons of the Most -High."* (Psalm 82:6-7) Every creature was created to reproduce according to their kind. Birds gives birth to bird, animals give birth to another animals. Fish give birth to fishes. When God create man, he created them in his own image.

However, if you don't know that you're a god, you shall die like men and fall like one of the princes the Bible says. Lack of knowledge put people at disadvantage in life. For example, Moses never knew that he was god until God told him. When God sent Moses to go back to pharaoh after being a fugitive in the wilderness, Moses was afraid of Pharaoh. God told him: "See, I have made you as a god to Pharaoh, and Aaron your brother shall be your prophet. (Exodus 7:1)

This knowledge empowered and emboldened Moses to confront Pharaoh with God's messages.

Chapter 12 : The Identity Keys That Break all Barriers

According to Bishop Abioye, he said, *"a Goat always gives birth to a baby Goat."* Since I am a child of God and I was made in the likeness of God, therefore, I am a god, and I will live like God.

Jesus also help us to know that we are gods when he quoted from the Book of Psalm above when he answered the Pharisees, "Is it not written in your law, *'I said, "You are gods" If He called them gods, to whom the word of God came and the Scripture cannot be broken.* **(John 10:34-35).**

At another occasion, Jesus encourages believers not to fear anyone who can only kill your body but cannot kill your soul. Rather fear Him who can destroy both soul and body in hell.

This means it is possible for a man to lose his body in death, without losing his spirit and soul. This knowledge will helped you to speak the truth at all times without fear of death, or fear of discipline. **(Matthew 10:28)**

Now that you have known your spiritual and physical identity this knowledge will assist you to speak like God.

You will love people like God. You will no longer be judgmental in your dealing with sinful men. You will have compassion for those who are the victim of an identity crisis.

Knowing your spiritual identity can propel you to success because you will know who you are and the purpose of God for life.

Spiritual Identity Key3

I am God's Child.

The second question is, what is your relationship with your Heavenly Father? Knowing that you were children of God and the evil one cannot touch you.

Chapter 12: The Identity Keys That Break all Barriers

You have the right to become God's children because of your faith in Christ Jesus. Your *faith in Jesus* you to be joint heirs with Jesus. Knowing that you are joint heirs to God' throne gives you confidence that your labor is not in vain. You will have no fear of Satan and his demons, and will not be afraid of what any man can do to you. **(John 1:12; 1 John 5:1,18; Romans 8: 14-15, 17).**

As a son or daughter of the Most High, God, your father is the owner of the world resource, and you will lack nothing good. God has a good plan for all his children in the beginning.

He made you rulers to dominate all other creatures, such as, the moving animals, the flying creatures, and the fishes in the sea. Also God put all the natural resources under your feet, such as water, cement, gold and silver, mineral oil and more.

Just like your natural parents, God wants the best for his children. For example, if you own all the flying birds in the world, how rich would you be?

Or if you are the owner of oil and gas under the soil, how rich would you be?

God said, in Jeremiah 29:11 *"For I know the thoughts that I think toward you, the thought of peace, and not of evil, to give you an expected end".*

(Proverb 22:4). This knowledge will help you to know that as a son or daughter of God you should never be poor.

Spiritual Identity Key 4

I am God's Temple, and His Spirit lives in me.

The best way possible to honor our creators is to take good care of our body because it is God's temple.

Chapter 12: The Identity Keys That Break all Barriers

God cannot live in concrete building like humans, therefore He lives in you as his sacred place of abode. You can imagine the hurt God feels when you decides to pollute your body and God's temple with drugs abuse, and alcohol addictions.

"Do you not know that your bodies are temples of the Holy Spirit, who is in you, whom you have received from God? You are not your own; you were bought at a price". Therefore honor God with your bodies". **(1 Corinthians 6:19-20)**

Apostle Paul further admonished:

"Do not be unequally yoked together with unbelievers. For what fellowship has righteousness with lawlessness? And what communion has light with darkness? And what accord has Christ with Belial? Or what part has a believer with an unbeliever? And what agreement has the temple of God with idols?

Know Your Spiritual Identity

For you is the temple of the living God. As God has said: "I will dwell in them And walk among them. I will be their God, And they shall be My people." Therefore "Come out from among them And be separate, says the Lord. Do not touch what is unclean, And I will receive you." "I will be a Father to you, And you shall be My sons and daughters, Says the Lord Almighty"(2 Corinthians 6:14-19)

You will not allow perversion, alcohol, drugs, and nicotine to pollute your body because it is God's Temple. The temporary enjoyment of sin has no place in your life anymore.

Holiness is your portion in the Name of Jesus.(1 Corinthians 3:16-17) This knowledge will help you to start treating your body as a Holy Place. Nicotine is unclean and a pollutant stop smoking. God will be happy with you if you stop smoking today.

Chapter 12 : The Identity Keys That Break all Barriers

Spiritual Identity Key 5

You Are Above All:

Since you are born of God, you have overcome the world. That means you are above sickness and you are above disease, failure, poverty, depression, frustration, miscarriage, barrenness, and others life problems.

"For whatever is born of God overcomes the world. And this is the victory that has overcome the world--our faith. Who is he who overcomes the world, but he who believes that Jesus is the Son of God"? **(1 John 5:4-5)**

You need to develop victory mentality in your new nature. God is a winner and does not know failure, you also as a son or daughter of God; you cannot afford to be a loser. (Ps. 82:6) Because you are gods, you carry the winning covenant mentality with God, the father. You have unlimited power to win, and there is no limit to what God can do to make you a winner.

God will bless those who bless you and curse those who curse you. "He said, your enemies will gather against you but they will fall for your sake, and no weapon form against you shall have any success. That is the heritage of the sons of God." **(Genesis 12:3; Isaiah 54:15, 17)**

God will not permit demons and its human agents, witches, and wizards to afflict you. He will do anything to protect you, even if it requires killing your enemies. You become an apple of His eyes.

You become untouchable. Your enemies will drink their blood and eat their flesh if they think of hurting you. Is that not comforting for you to know that God is your protection?

For thus says the Lord of hosts: "He sent me after glory, to the nations which plunder

Chapter 12 : The Identity Keys That Break all Barriers

you; for he who touches you touches the apple of His eye".

"For surely I will shake my hand against them, and they shall become spoils for their servants. Then you will know that the Lord of hosts has sent me." **(Zachariah 2: 8-9; Isaiah 49:24-26)**

Spiritual Identity Key 6

I Dominated My Circumstances

Then God said, "Let us make mankind in our image, in our likeness, so that they may rule over the fish in the sea and the birds in the sky, over the livestock and all the wild animals, and over all the creatures that move along the ground." (Genesis 1:26) God created us in His likeness, and he made us gods to dominate our circumstances in life and to rule over other creatures he had created.

Know Your Spiritual Identity

You will be dominating sickness, dominating poverty, disease, witches, and wizards, and all things are under my feet. Why should you be fearful of anything? For example, I never knew my spiritual identity when I was serving the Watchtower Society until I come to Jesus who liberated me from them. I know my rights and obligation as a son of God.

No evil power can dominate my life again in the mighty name of Jesus. You too can be free from fear of men and falsehood. Never again would I be intimidated by any circumstances in the Mighty Name of Jesus. **Amen.**

Spiritual Identity Key7

I have been Anointed and sealed by God.

"For all the promises of God in Him are Yes, and in Him Amen,

Chapter 12 : The Identity Keys That Break all Barriers

to the glory of God through us. Now He who establishes us with you in Christ and has anointed us is God, who also has sealed us and given us the Spirit in our hearts as a guarantee"(II Corinthians 1:21-23).

God has called you by anointing you and by sealing you so that you can be useful to him, benefit yourself, and to become a blessing to your generations. God established you in Christ and has anointed you and has sealed you by Holy Spirit, so that you can become a joint heir with Jesus. "For as many as are led by the Spirit of God, these are sons of God and children, then heirs—heirs of God and joint heirs with Christ, if indeed we suffer from Him, that we may also be glorified together".(Romans 8:14, 17). If you know that you are a joint heir with Jesus in his heavenly Kingdom, how would that knowledge change your behavior? If you are convincing that God has anointed you to rule with his son in

Know Your Spiritual Identity

Heaven or on Earth would that give you a reason to respect yourself and your maker? Certainly knowing your spiritual identity in Christ will reflect in the way you live your life. You will live your life to please your creator and you will locate God purpose for your life and fulfill your destiny.

The United States of America, President Trump was talking about the power of prayers and salvation through Jesus Christ! He called out John Pounder from Las Vegas, Navada as a good example. He said, "John grew up without a father. He joined Street Gangs and live a life of criminal. He was in and out of jail until the age of 38 years old. While in federal prison he listens to the Family Radio program by Reverend Bill Gram. He heard that Jesus wants to be the Lord of your life. That day John gave his life to Jesus and he started reading the Bible and meditating on the Scriptures.

Chapter 12: The Identity Keys That Break all Barriers

Today John runs a ministry that helps more than two thousand prison inmates. John is a living testimony to the power of prayer that nothing is more important than God", the president said.

What happens is that God performed a spiritual surgical operation on John, by removing the wicked hearts of stone and replacing it with a new heart flesh, and a new spirit (Ezekiel 36:26). The point is if you think your situation is far worse and there is no more hope for you, pause a minute and know that there is nothing too difficult for God. Just give God a chance to redeem your life from all the vices of the devil. Having a personal relationship with God and knowing your spiritual identity in Christ will free you from crisis of your life. Jesus said," all things are possible to him/her that believes" (Mark 9:23)

Know Your Spiritual Identity

Spiritual Identity Key 8

I am God's family.

"Now, therefore, you are no longer strangers and foreigners, but fellow citizens with the saints and members of the household of God, having been built on the foundation of the apostles and prophets, Jesus Christ Himself being the chief cornerstone". (Ephesians 2:19-20 NKJV

As a family of God, you are not inferior to any human race. You are a citizen of God's Heavenly Kingdom. You belong to the household of God with the apostles and prophets of God with Jesus Christ as your brother. The Bible says, if you walk according the rule, peace and mercy will be upon you and you shall become the Israel of God.

You will also have a dual citizenship of Heaven even though you are a citizen of your country. You will proudly say, "I am a citizen of Heaven, and I am a joint heir with Jesus". You shall be entitled to God's blessings because you are a product of His grace.

This knowledge will help you to know that your race or nationality has no bearing on your destiny. **(Galatians 6:16, Philippians 3:20).**

Spiritual Identity Key9

I have been declared righteous.

Jesus said:

"There is no condemnation for those who are putting faith in Christ Jesus because through Christ Jesus the law of the Spirit who gives life has set you free from the law of sin and death." **(Romans 8:1-2)**

Presently your sinful flesh is producing sickness and death because everyone will reap whatever they sowed. Anyone who sows to the pleasing of flesh will certainly go down into grave.

Roman 6:23 says the wages of sin is death. If you allow sin to be your employer, the only wages to expect from Satan is death. However Jesus is giving you a different law of the spirit. The law of the spirit will give you everlasting life. Your past sins are forgiven and blotted out.

You have been declared righteous by Jesus who paid for your past sins, and paid for your present sins, and paid for your future sins based on grace alone.

Therefore, since you have been declared righteous through faith, you have peace with God through our Lord Jesus Christ. (**Luke 15:7, 10**)

The Angels are rejoicing in the Heaven because you give your life to Jesus. Jesus will give you a fresh start in life. You will have a clear conscience, and you shall be

Chapter 12: The Identity Keys That Break all Barriers

free to approach your father in Heaven without the feeling of being condemned. May God continually give you the grace of obedience and the fear of the Lord, in the name of Jesus? Amen

Spiritual Identity Key10

I am in union with the Lord.

Jesus said:

"I no longer call you servants because a servant does not know his master's business. Instead, I have called you friends, for everything that I learned from my Father I have made known to you".**(John 15:15)**

Whoever is union with the Lord is one with him in spirit. Now you are the body of Christ, and each one of you is a part of it. The Lord and you have become one body just as Jesus and his father have become one.

That was why you would not join your body with prostitutes. You will not sleep

Know Your Spiritual Identity

with animals and you will flee from any form of perversions. You will not pollute your body with drugs, and alcohol, and with nicotine.

If you trust Jesus as your friend and that he will always be by your side and protect you, you will do everything and anything to earn his trust. You will not go back to drugs and alcohol, and perversion, and betray your friend, Jesus Christ. *"He that is jointed unto the LORD is one spirit"* **(1 Corinthians 6:17)**.

You will join your body to Jesus, who will clean you from all infirmities that resulted from your previous life. Knowing your spiritual identity in Christ will give you faith in Jesus, strong faith that can draw power of miracle from Jesus to clean you. I pray for you today: Receive power to become clean in the mighty name of Jesus. **Amen.**

Chapter 12: The Identity Keys That Break all Barriers

Spiritual Identity Key11

Jesus redeems me

"In him, I have redemption through his blood, the forgiveness of sins, following the riches of God's grace that he lavished on me. With all wisdom and understanding, he made known to us the mystery of his will according to his good pleasure, which he purposed in Christ" **(Ephesians 1:7-9)**

Knowledge is power. Knowing your spiritual identity in Christ has given you the power of redemption. Anyone the son has set free, he or she is free indeed. You shall be free entirely in the mighty name of Jesus.

Jesus has rescued you from the dominion of darkness and brought us into the kingdom of the Son he loves, in which you have redemption, the forgiveness of sins **(Colossians 1:13-14).**

Know Your Spiritual Identity

The following testimony of a hopeless drug addict is a testimony of how God can deliver you from destruction. "I was a chronic alcoholic, cocaine, crack, and a chain pot and cigarette smoker. I was hospitalized three times for alcohol overdose.

I have been fighting this demon for several years. For eleven and a half months, I was living on the street. I had reached a breaking point when I was put out of the shelter and was robbed two times at gunpoint. I have nothing left than the cloth on my back, and I cry to God to help me.

That was when God sent Pastor David from Jesus Witness Ministries to help me. I have been clean from drugs and alcohol addiction for more than three months. Presently, I am working, I have a roof over my head, and my wife is coming back to me."**(GS testifier)**

Chapter 12: The Identity Keys That Break all Barriers

Spiritual Identity Key12

Everlasting Life is a gift

There is no doubt that we are living at the time of the end of this wicked generation. Presently everything God gave us for free is been commercialized. For example, people are been made to pay for their salvation with money and with work.

You may be hearing some men of God are telling their congregation that they need to pay their tithes before they can make heaven, and that their tithes and offering is their passport to heaven. Other will say, you are not entitled to God blessing if you fail to pay your tithes. Or the more you give your time and money to their Church, the more God will bless you in return.

If that is true, it means that it is only those who can pay their tithes and offering will qualify for heavenly Kingdom.

However what the Bible say contradicts what these people are saying.

Apostle Paul says:

"For it is by grace you have been saved, through faith—and this is not from yourselves, it is the gift of God— not by works, so that no one can boast" **(Ephesians 2:8-9)**.

Developing a personal relationship with God and knowing your spiritual identity has given you the knowledge not to pay again for everlasting life.

It is a gift. Jesus is the only mediator between God and man. Therefore, no false prophet can rob you of your resources. God can hear your prayers without a false prophet.

You can confidently go directly to God. Knowing your spiritual identity is the key to freedom from false prophets who promises

Chapter 12 : The Identity Keys That Break all Barriers

riches to their member, while enriching only their-selves.

Spiritual Identity Key13

Jesus replied:

"Anyone who loves me will obey my teaching. My Father will love them, and we will come to them and make our home with them." **(John 14:23).**

Your past is past. Presently you are a new creation. God is using your new person. The only way to show that you want Jesus to live in your heart and that God should live with you is for you to obey and comply with God requirements.

I am inviting you to come to Jesus for salvation, and to have a new beginning with Christ. *This knowledge helped you to clean your environment because your heavenly father and Jesus will not live in a dirty place. You have to be spiritually and physically clean.* There is nothing impossible for God. He can change the corrupt mind and body and can re-create a new person in you. You will forever be free from condemnation.

The Angels in Heaven will rejoice over you and God will adopt you as son/daughter. Jesus said, "I tell you that in the same way there will be more rejoicing in heaven over one sinner who repents than over ninety-nine righteous persons who do not need to repent" (Luke 15:7)

"Moreover whom He predestined these He also called; whom God called, these He also justified. Whom he justified, this, He also glorified. Who shall bring a charge against God's elect? It is God who justifies. (Romans 8:30, 33 NKJV).

Therefore you should not be judging anyone God had declared righteous. **Don't**

Chapter 12: The Identity Keys That Break all Barriers

give up. *Winners don't quit, and quitters don't win.* This is one of the solutions to spiritual identity crisis. You shall win the battle of your life in the mighty name of Jesus. **(Romans 8:12)**

Spiritual Identity Key 14

I am a citizen of Heaven.

"For our citizenship is in heaven, from which we eagerly wait for the Savior, the Lord Jesus Christ, who will transform our lowly body that it may be conformed to His glorious body, according to the working by which He is able even to subdue all things to Himself" **(Philippians 3:20-21).**

Who is a citizen you may asked?

A citizen is a native or naturalized member of a nation who owes allegiance to its government and is entitled to its protection.

Know Your Spiritual Identity

Dr. Myles Monroe defined citizenship as *"the constitutional rights and privileges bestowed upon an individual, guaranteeing legal status to the individual, who is protected by the laws of the country."* There is no greater honor can be given to an individual than the recognition or making him or her citizen.

For example, I have dual citizenship. I was born as a citizen of Nigeria, and I became a naturalized citizen of America.

I do not know the value of citizenship until I moved to the United States of America. So many people spend close to 20 years before having the privileges of becoming a citizen.

To become a citizen, you have to pledge allegiance to your host country, follow the constitution and pay your taxes whenever it is due. Then you are entitled to have equal

Chapter 12: The Identity Keys That Break all Barriers

rights of protection and other privileges' that the law bestowed on the citizen.

Similarly, as a born-again Christian, or as a citizen of Heaven, you are empowered to access all the rights and the privileges of the Kingdom Government constitution (the Bible).

Your citizenship enables you to call the constitutional opportunities and promises. The law constitution is more potent than the citizen, just as the law is more powerful than the judges or lawyers. Citizenship is the most powerful gift a citizen can get from the government. Nationality is a covenant relationship between a citizen and the host government.

For example, human government demands taxes. God demands 10% Tithes during the time of Moses. With a promise to open the heavenly blessings to bless you and to rebuke devourers for your sake (Malachi 3:10-11).

Jesus demands sowing of hundred percent seed as kingdom investment like the widow who gave all she has.

"The fruit of the Spirit is love, joy, peace, longsuffering, kindness, goodness, faithfulness, gentleness, self-control. As such, there is no law. Moreover, those who are Christ's have crucified the flesh with its passions and desires, If we live in the Spirit, let us also walk in the Spirit **(Galatia 5:22-24)**.

As a citizen of God's Kingdom, you're expected to obey the Heavenly rules and regulations and to bear the fruits of the Holy Spirit in other to keep your citizenship. ***What are the rules you may ask?***

One of them is Love because God is love. Anyone who does not have love cannot be a citizen of God's government. Joy is the

Chapter 12: The Identity Keys That Break all Barriers

quality like perfume people are using today to smell good.

You must radiate joy, and your happiness must saturate your environment at all times. Then be peaceable with all people because you cannot see God without peace and holiness. Long-suffering and gentleness is our character and behavior as a citizen of Heaven. In God's kingdom discrimination is forbidden.

Faith is another fruit of God's Holy Spirit, and without hope, you cannot be in God's kingdom. God is looking for meek and humble people to promote and appoint them to rule with Jesus in Heaven, if you are arrogant don't apply.

The only required qualification is humility plus the above qualities and self-control. Self-control is a body part in humans like a break in the automobile. If your car does not have a break can you drive it safely? The answer is no. Self-control is a human control part that you will need as a citizen of God's kingdom. Jesus is the King of God's Heavenly Government, and He is ready to assist you to develop Godly qualities of Love, Peace, Joy, Longsuffering, gentleness, goodness, faith, meekness and self-control.

There is no law above these in the God's constitution- Bible. As a citizen of Heaven, living on earth, the Holy Spirit will give you the gift of the spirit to live above what is common to an earthly man.

For example, a citizen of Heavenly Government has the power and the authority to preach the good news about the Christ Kingdom. You have the rights to use Jesus name to cast out demons and to heal the sick. You have the rights to enjoy the spiritual prosperity of good health, peace and security, riches, glory and the grace of everlasting life.(I Corinthian 12:8-11; Mark

Chapter 12: The Identity Keys That Break all Barriers

16: 17-18; Luke 10:19-20; Prov. 22:4; Exeo. 23:25-26)

As human government has law enforcement officers to enforce the laws, God also allow Satan to accuse people whenever they break God's laws. For example, I made a vow to God twenty year before, that I would serve him fulltime at age sixty but I forgot completely.

When I became age sixty-two, I was laid off from my job, and *I was wondering why?*

Then God brought it to my memory about my vow. I knew Satan must have reminded God of my failing to fulfill my vow. God allows Satan to enforce the law. Satan accuses us before our God whenever we sin or miss the mark of perfection.

It is in our best interest not to give Satan any legal rights to afflict us in any way **(Revelation 12:10).**

Know Your Spiritual Identity

"For as many as are led by the Spirit of God, these are sons/daughter of God, and if children, then heirs—heirs of God and joint heirs with Christ, if indeed we suffer from Him, that we may also be glorified together." **(Romans 8:14, 17)**

Jesus promised to come back to take home many people who qualify to be a citizen of Heaven. Is there a limit to those who can become a citizen of Heaven? As many, as received Him, to them He gave the right to become children of God, to those who believe in His name: who were born, not of blood, nor of the will of the flesh, nor of the will of man, but of God. **(John 1:12; 1John 5:1; Revelation 19:1)**

The above-quoted Scriptures show that there is no limit to the number of those who qualify to become the citizen of God's Kingdom and become God's children. All citizens have equal rights and obligations in a country; similarly, all God's children have equal chances or equal rights to rule in Heaven with Jesus Christ.

It is not the business of any person or religion organization to class people to either heaven or earth. God has the ultimate rights to select anyone he chooses to be a joint ruler with his son, Jesus Christ whether in Heaven or on Earth (Acts 1:6

Fear Eliminated Key15

The Bible says:

"God has not given us a spirit of fear but of power and love and a sound mind. (2 Timothy 1:7) For you did not receive the spirit of bondage again to fear, but you received the Spirit of adoption by whom we cry out, "Abba, Father." **(Romans 8:14-15)**

Fear is a distressing emotion aroused by impending danger, evil, pain, whether the threat is real or imagined. Some psychologist described fear as a false expectation appearing real.

That means, if the sense of dread did not come from God, it came from Satan. To me, fear is a demonic messenger or bait of the devil to lure faint hearted people before afflicting them with problems. Pastor Alero described fear as a "spirit of insanity". Job acknowledged the negative power of fear when he said,

"What I feared has come upon me; what I dreaded has happened to me. I have no peace, no quietness; I have no rest, but only turmoil." **(Job 3:25, 26 NIV)**

Job lost ten children in a matter of one week because he was afraid of something may happen to his children. This fear made him to be making sacrifices to God to avert disaster over his children.

Any fear that is holding you hostage be cast out in the mighty name of Jesus. You

Chapter 12: The Identity Keys That Break all Barriers

got the Power, not Fear. Fear is the conduit by which demonic power flows through, whereas Faith is the conduit by which God's power flow through, noted by Jentezen Franklin.

Pastor Jentezen Franklin narrated his experience while traveling on the airplane. He said, "Immediately after serving lunch, the pilot announced that they are entering dangerous stormy weather.

As the plane was descending and ascending, other passengers are crying and shouting, he was busy eating his launch. He reasoned, *"even if that will be the end of his physical life, he will not go to God with an empty stomach."*

He was not afraid of death. Coward died before their actual death. Thank God the plane landed safely.

Know Your Spiritual Identity

The spirit of God led God's children to freedom, but the spirit of fear leads people to bondage.

You have an option to either choose the spirit of fear that leads to bondage or God's spirit which leads to freedom. Joshua told the Israelites, "Do not be afraid, nor be dismayed; be strong and be of good courage, for thus the LORD will do to all your enemies against whom you fight." **(Joshua 10:25 NKJV)**

No coward can please God. Faint-Heartedness is a sin to God. That is why God listed coward person among the sexually immoral persons and liars. These sins carried a capital punishment of everlasting death. God revealed this to Apostles John, in the book of revelation, those who shall be totally cut-off, when he said, "But the cowardly, unbelieving, abominable, murderers, sexually immoral, sorcerers, idolaters, and all liars shall have their part in the lake which burns with fire and brimstone, which is the second death." **(Revelation 21:8 NKJV)**

No weapon formed against you shall prosper, and every tongue which rises against you in judgment you shall condemn. This is the heritage of the servants of the LORD, and their righteousness is from me," Says the LORD. **(Isaiah 54:17 NKJV)**

While the fear of men leads to a snare. The fear of demon leads to bondage. Fear is sinful because it lacks faith. Knowing your spiritual identity in Christ eliminates fear from your life. Fear is a demonic messenger. Therefore be courageous and be faithful to the end. God rewards only the fearless.

Spiritual Identity Key16

Godly Fear bring Blessing

The fear of God is the idea of living in respect, awe, and submission to a deity. The first mention of the fear of God. "Fear the Lord, you his holy people, for those who fear him lack nothing.

The lions may grow weak and hungry, but those who seek the Lord lack no good thing". That means the only acceptable and profitable fear is the fear of the true God. "The fear of the LORD is the beginning of wisdom: and the knowledge of the holy is understanding (Proverb 9:10." Proverb 22:4) that humility and the fear of true God lead to riches, honor, and life.

Spiritual Identity Key17

Jesus invited people for freedom

Jesus invited all lovers of freedom and sincere truth seekers, when he said:

"Come to me, all YOU who are toiling and loaded down, and I will refresh YOU. Take my yoke upon YOU and learn from me,

Chapter 12: The Identity Keys That Break all Barriers

for I am mild-tempered and lowly in heart, and YOU will find refreshment for YOUR souls. For my yoke is kindly and my load is light." **(Matthew 11:28-29).**

"Now Jehovah is the Spirit; and where the spirit of Jehovah is, there is freedom."

The above quoted Scriptures show that demonic agents, the false prophets and hypocrites has have beating God's children down with heavy loads, demanding people to pay for their salvation and to buy God's blessings. It is the knowledge of God and your position in God's arrangement that will give you the power to be free from false prophets.

It is refreshing to know that everlasting life is free because Jesus paid for it. However, Satan can make you pay again if you are ignorant of your identity in Christ. Demonic agent load is heavy. For example, those who want to become rich at all cost usually fall prey to the devil.

The fake prophets may say to the people, if you want to be a millionaire come out and those who are greedy will be asked to give $1,000 or more. Some witch doctor may demand the sacrifices of their victim best son, or their body part for sacrifice.

These are heavy load on the people. Jesus load is light; it is based on grace alone. It is not based on your money, service, or work, so that no one can boast.

During Jesus earthly ministry he attended Jewish Temples and Synagogues; he found that the religious leaders are the hypocrite just like religious leaders of today. Jesus recruited commercial fisher men, Doctors, Lawyers and ordinary people to be his disciples. He gave them the power to preach about God's Kingdom and to cast out

Chapter 12: The Identity Keys That Break all Barriers

demons and to heal the sick in all part of the world.

Moreover, God commanded us to congregate with other fellow believers to praise and worship him. How can we fulfill this sacred obligation without been misled by false prophets? **(Hebrew 10:24,25)**

Our Lord recommended Bible fellowship when he said: *"Truly I say to YOU men, whatever things YOU may bind on earth will be things bound in heaven, and whatever things YOU may loose on earth will be things loosed in heaven. Again I truly say to YOU, if two of YOU on earth agree concerning anything of importance that they should request, it will take place for them due to my Father in heaven. "For where there are two or three gathered together in my name, there I am in their midst."* **(Mathew 18:18-20)**

Know Your Spiritual Identity

Jesus demonstrated that you don't need mega churches or a big Cathedral to serve God acceptably. You don't need big Church to be safe. He himself got out of the traditional religion of his parent,(Judaism religion) and gave power to believers to carry out God's assignment to preach God message to the world for a witness before the end of this wicked generation end. For example, Jesus has performed many healing such as Cancers, Glaucoma, and other miracles and deliverance in our ministry with fewer members.

One example was in December 2016 a sister wants me to pray for her mother. The mother was sick with stage four Lung Cancer. When she told me that her mother was a chain smoker and she doesn't attend churches.

At hearing this, I was reluctant to pray for her but the daughter was crying, that

Chapter 12 : The Identity Keys That Break all Barriers

she believes that if I pray, God will heal her mother. Jesus reminded me that the faith of her daughter is enough to heal her mother. After the prayer, the mother was taken for the scan test as a final test before the lung replacement surgery. The hospital staffs did not find cancer in the woman anymore. Jesus eliminated lung Cancer from the mother. Her daughter was jubilating about the miracle Jesus performed. I was shocked.

I asked the daughter to take me to see the mother. When I met the woman, she was cured of lung cancer. She told me that the Doctor's were shocked and they ask her to come back in two weeks for more tests. They did not know that Jesus is still healing people today. There is power in the name of Jesus.

Knowing your spiritual identity will give you the power to cast out demons and to heal the sick.

Know Your Spiritual Identity

Apostle Paul further said:

"For such freedom, Christ set us free. Therefore stand fast, and do not let yourselves be confined again in a yoke of slavery."(Galatians 5:1) Jesus further said, "You will know the truth, and the truth will set You free. Anyone the son set free, he is free indeed." **(John 8:32, 36)**.

Your identity in Christ, and personal relationship with Jesus Christ is more important than your religious activities.

Spiritual Identity Key18

Prayer for freedom from fear

PRAYER POINT

1) Father please set me free from the bondage of fear of intimidation in the name of Jesus.
2) Jesus Eliminates Fear of excommunication and shunning in the mighty name of Jesus.

Chapter 12: The Identity Keys That Break all Barriers

3) Holy Ghost Fire and the blood of Jesus arise to destroy all forms of oppression, suppression, and coercion, in the Mighty Name of Jesus.

4) Holy Ghost Fire delivers me from the bondage of fear of men, fear of witches, and fear of demons, in the mighty name of Jesus.

5) Father removes the Fear of men, fear of human organization and the fear of death in the mighty name of Jesus.

6) Father frees me from all form of perversion, drugs and alcohol in the mighty name of Jesus.

7) Father delivers me from all bondage of fear that is tormenting my life in the mighty name of Jesus.

8) Holy Ghost Fire and the Blood of Jesus ARISE and destroy depression, torment, and pain in my life in the name of Jesus.

9) Father empowers me with perfect LOVE, Power and Sound Mind in the Mighty Name of Jesus.

Jesus said,

"In My name, they will cast out demons; they will speak with new tongues, they will

Know Your Spiritual Identity

take up serpents, and if they drink anything deadly, it will by no means hurt them, they will lay hands on the sick, and they will recover." **(Mark 16:15, 17-18).**

Your spiritual identity in Christ will be eliminating fear from your life. *Praise the living Jesus!*

I did not experience God's miraculous power when I was a member of Jehovah's witnesses.

In January 2019 I was informed about three young people from three different States, USA, that they were afflicted with the spirit of insanity.

I prayed to Jesus to cast out the spirit of insanity from them. Jesus responded by eliminating evil spirit from them and these young women has resume their normal duties to the *Glory of the LORD*.

Chapter 12 : The Identity Keys That Break all Barriers

The Bible says oppose the devil and it will flee from you. Jesus said, *"However, this kind does not go out except by prayer and fasting"* **(Mathew 17:21).**

This means you need to have close relationship with Jesus Christ and follow his instructions.

Spiritual Identity Key19

I AM SIGNIFICANT:

In other to be a salt of the earth, you must know who you are and know your identity in Christ Jesus. This knowledge will help you to discover your destiny and how to fulfill it. You are the light of the world and your light will beam to the world and you will be a blessing to your generation. The few people who discovered their destiny early in life and they are fulfilling their God's ordained plan for their lives, are most successful people in the world.

Know Your Spiritual Identity

You find these people in business, science and technology and in the ministry of God. This knowledge helped you to value your reputation among people because you are the salt of the world.

You should not lose your salt by allowing drugs and alcohol, and perversion, and immorality to damage your reputation. Jesus is counting on you to be the light of the world, and to be the salt to your generation.

I am the salt and the light of the world.

"You are the salt of the earth; but if the salt loses its flavor, how shall it be seasoned? It is then good for nothing but to be thrown out and trampled underfoot by men. "You are the light of the world. A city that is set on a hill cannot be hidden." **(Matthew 5:13-14)**

Chapter 12: The Identity Keys That Break all Barriers

Spiritual Identity 20

I bear Witness to Jesus.

Jesus said:

"You shall receive power when the Holy Spirit has come upon you, and you shall be witnesses to Me in Jerusalem, and in all Judea and Samaria, and to the end of the earth." **(Acts 1:8)**

"Go therefore and make disciples of all the nations, baptizing them in the name of the Father and of the Son and the Holy Spirit, teaching them to observe all things that I have commanded you; and lo, I am with you always, even to the end of the age." **(Matthew 28:19-20)**

Many people today make excuses that God did not call them to preach the word and win soul for God's Kingdom.

The truth is all believers are called and you are anointed to bear fruits for God's

Kingdom. Jesus at the end of his early ministries sent a helper to interpret many things that were not yet understood by Jesus early disciples. The Holy Spirit serves as an advocate and a witness to Jesus. Jesus further said, the Holy Spirit testified about me, and you also will bear witness, because you have been with me from the beginning. **(John 15: 16, 27)**

The Angels are My Co-Workers. The Angels in Heaven are supporting me to bear witness to Jesus because they too are Jesus Witnesses. Jesus said, "I have sent my angel to testify to you these things in the churches.

I am the Root and the Offspring of David, the Bright and Morning Star." **(Revelation 22:16)** Moreover, I fell at his feet to worship him. However, he said to me, "See that you do not do that! I am your fellow servant, and of your brethren who

Chapter 12: The Identity Keys That Break all Barriers

have the testimony of Jesus. Worship God! *"For the testimony of Jesus is the spirit of prophecy."* **(Revelation 19:10)**

I derived my joy from bearing witness to Jesus. I will be miserable without witnessing to Christ Jesus. Join me at Jesus Witness Ministries. My happiness and prayers are that all people should come to Jesus for Salvation, for healing and for deliverance.

My goal is to win a million souls for Christ every year until Jesus come. We need to raise a people who will form the citizen of God's Kingdom. I hope to accomplish this through social media and support from people like you.

Please join me to bear witness to the glory of Jesus.

Know Your Spiritual Identity

Spiritual Identity Key22

I am a minister of reconciliation:

Paul made this clear to me when he wrote to the Ephesians Congregation in Chapter 3:12,

"Now all things are of God, who has reconciled us to Himself through Jesus Christ and has given us the ministry of reconciliation, that is, that God was in Christ reconciling the world to Him, not imputing their trespasses to them, and has committed to us the word of reconciliation. **(II Corinthians 5:18-19)**

In whom we have boldness and access with confidence through faith in Him". **(Ephesians 3:12)**

What is reconciliation?

Reconciliation means to bring something in alignment or to bring two warring party

Chapter 12 : The Identity Keys That Break all Barriers

together in peace. All men have sinned from the Garden of Eden through disobedience to their creator. Men have deviated from God purpose for our lives.

God's plan for your lives is to make you a ruler over all the creative work of God. In the third John 2, the Bible says, "Beloved, I wish above all things that thou may prosper and be in health, even as thy soul proper".

Also, God want his children to be in wealth and to be in health. On the other hands, Satan introduced perversion, confusion, drugs and alcohol, nicotine, false religion, wars, and persecution of believers into the world. The Bible say, "the wages of sin is death"(Roman 6:23).

How can you be appointed to be a minister of reconciliation? You want to clean your lives and make yourself available, so that God can appoint you as a minister of reconciliation.

Know Your Spiritual Identity

Your job is to preach the word of salvation, faith, and forgiveness of sin to people in your neighborhood. Jesus shall pick you if you know your spiritual identity in Christ Jesus. Know your spiritual identity is one of the keys to be reconciled to God.

Spiritual Identity Key25

The Power of the Holy Spirit:

"For the kingdom of God is not in word but in power. (I Corinthians 4:20 NKJV) For our gospel did not come to you in word only, but also in power, and in the Holy Spirit and much assurance, as you know what kind of men we were among you for your sake". (I Thessalonians 1:5)

The Holy Spirit will give you the power to overcome perversions and drugs addictions. Holy Spirit is the third part of God. He is the most important person in the universe. He was co-creator when God is

Chapter 12 : The Identity Keys That Break all Barriers

creating the earth. He conceived the natural birth of Jesus.

He resurrected Jesus Christ from the grave. God is a spirit, and the Holy Spirit is God. Holy Spirit is the power of God and appears in different forms. He can like the electricity in your house that has various uses. You can iron your clothes, watch your TV, drive your train, fly your planes, and it can display different colors. Similarly, the Holy Spirit is dynamic, and it can be useful in various forms and a different situation.

Jesus introduced the Holy Spirit as a person that will continue his salvation ministries. One of his duties is to write God's laws and regulations into your hearts so that you will not need anyone to teach how to serve your God. He will help you to understand your spiritual identity in Jesus as the LORD. **(Hebrew 10:15-17)**

He will distribute spiritual gifts to all men of God and asks you to bear the fruits of God's Holy Spirits in your daily lives. The Holy Spirit will reveal to you the solutions to your spiritual identity crisis in your lives. **(John 15:25-27)**

Jesus further said:

"You shall receive power when the Holy Spirit has come upon you, and you shall be witnesses to Me in Jerusalem, and in all Judea and Samaria, and to the end of the earth." **(Acts 1:8)**

There is power in the name of Jesus. I am using this power Jesus gave me to preach the good news and to free people from the demonic bondage of fear, falsehood, drugs and alcohol addictions and to heal the sick in the Mighty Name of Jesus.

For example, on April 12, 2013, I heard a woman shouting, "Holy Ghost Fire my

Chapter 12 : The Identity Keys That Break all Barriers

daughter don die o". I heard only fire and I ran out of my apartment, I saw my neighbor with her three-year-old daughter lifeless.

As I was shouting to the mother, take the dead child to the Hospital, I heard a powerful commanding voice of Jesus, and He said, "Take the baby from the mother. Place her on your arm. Lay her on the couch. Call her name three times, and I will wake her up." I took the baby from the mother as commanded and following the LORD instructions.

On the third time that I called the baby's name, the baby sneezed three times. I said, open your eyes, she opened her eyes, I said again, give me your hands, and she gave me her hands. I commanded, stand up, and she stood up. And I handed her over to her mother. That baby girl is almost ten years old now, and they live in my neighborhood. *May all glory be to Jesus Christ.!!*

Know Your Spiritual Identity

Another testimony was a young boy in my church who was under the oppression of the devil. He has violent autistic behavior. All regular school rejected him. His parent took him to a special education school, two hours away from his school district. The mother approach me with the problem because she knows that God is using me as a vessel for healing and deliverance.

I prayed to Jesus to heal this boy, and he recommends that the boy be given a new name, the parent complied with divine instructions. After the name changed the boy was healed supernaturally. That boy has recovered and is doing great at a regular high school. May all the glory be to Jesus.

These testimonies are so much for this book. Jesus said, "I know my sheep, and they hear my voice, and they follow me." I have had the privilege of hearing Jesus voice occasionally. At each time, miracle does

Chapter 12 : The Identity Keys That Break all Barriers

happen. I appreciate Jesus for using me as a vessel for healing and deliverance.

You too shall be a vessel for honorable purpose in the mighty name of Jesus. Amen. Jesus knew who he was. He said I am the son of God. I am the true light. I am the son of Man. I am the vine. I am the door of the sheep. I am the way. I am the truth. I am the life. Jesus was able to conquer the world of Satan because he knew his true identity. Bishop Abioye said, *"If you're confused about who you're, Satan will declare you who you are not."*

Declaration of your identity is the beginning of the restoration of your dignity". When I know that I am a conqueror, I was able to conquer my enemies. I have dominion over my circumstances because God said so. The day I realized that my father is the owner of world resources, I declare that "I will never be poor again" with due apology to Bishop Oyedepo.

I testify to the glory of God. The day I know that my spiritual father's and Jesus don't wear eyeglasses. I was grieved in my spirit and cry to God to give me new eyes. God answer my prayers, and that was the last time I wore glasses after more than 25 years of wearing glasses.

May Jesus take all the glory. Jesus is the same yesterday, today and forever. **(Hebrew 13:8)**

Spiritual Key #26

The Key to Fruitfulness:

There are different keys to open different doors. There are spiritual keys and there are physical keys. The spiritual keys can open physical doors.

There is key to marital fruitfulness and there is key to financial fruitfulness.

Chapter 12: The Identity Keys That Break all Barriers

Many problems can be overcome when you know the spiritual solutions to those problems. For example, if a woman cannot conceive after two years of marriage and there is no fruit of the womb, then there is a problem.

The problem may not only be biological issues. It may be due to lack of knowing the key to marital fruitfulness.

When God blessed the first human, God said, "be fruitful and populate the earth". Any bareness is not from God. It is an error under the sun. God did not create anything, from plants to animals to be barren or to be unfruitful. God said, *"You shall be blessed above all peoples; there shall not be a male or female barren among you or among your livestock"* **(Deuteronomy 7:14)**

Therefore, knowing the spiritual key of marital fruitfulness is very important to be delivered from bareness. What is the key to marital fruitfulness? Just as I said earlier, there is spiritual fruitfulness and there is marital fruitfulness.

The spiritual fruitfulness precedes the physical fruitfulness. Jesus said, any branch that does not bear fruit, he cut off. And the one that bear fruits he prune it so that, it can be more fruitful.

In John 15:2, 16 Jesus made it clear that you should go and bear fruits-(win souls for God). After that, whatever, you ask the father in my name; He may give it to you. This means bearing spiritual fruits and children is the first step to bearing the marital fruits of the womb (children). This is the key to fruitfulness.

This spiritual key to fruitfulness is also re-echo in the Book of Exodus 23:25-26 when the Bible says, you must serve the Lord your God and He will bless your food

Chapter 12 : The Identity Keys That Break all Barriers

and water and take away sickness from your midst. And no one will be barren in your midst. God can remove all sickness whether it is fibroid nor hormonal imbalance or low egg or no sperm.

There are many people who have discovered this spiritual key to fruitfulness and they have given testimonies of how they devoted their time and resources to put God first in their lives and the yoke of bareness was broken in their lives.

It is my candid opinion that if anyone is not bearing marital seed, let her engage fully in wining soul for God or serving God in other areas and then God will be committed to remember her as he remember Ana and Sarah.

CHAPTER 13
PRAYERS OF DELIVERANCE

Jesus said, the word that I spoke to you is life and is spirit. Every word of God carries divine code or secret to solve life problems. You will know the truth about your identity in Christ and the truth will make you free from immorality, perversion, fear and falsehood.

Anyone the son make free, is free indeed. Therefore there is power in the name of Jesus to cast out demonic powers in your life.

Jesus said…..

"It is the Spirit who gives life; the flesh profits nothing. The words that I speak to you are spirit, and they are life." **John 6:63**

The power of God to deliver you resides in his words because his words are spirit,

Chapter 13 : Prayers of Deliverance

and they are life. Jesus uses the same word to heal and deliver many people from their disease and demonic powers.

Psalm 107:19-20 says: "Then they cried out to the Lord in their trouble, and He saved them out of their distresses. He sent His word and healed them, and delivered them from their destructions".

There is no condition God can not reverse. His word can deliver you from any depraved condition you find yourself. You need to take a step of faith and cry to God in prayers and eat his word like food and you shall be delivered.

In John 8: 32, 34, 36: "And you shall know the truth, and the truth shall make you free. Jesus answered them, "Most assuredly, I say to you, whoever commits sin is a slave of sin. Therefore if the Son makes you free, you shall be free indeed"

Know Your Spiritual Identity

The above Scriptures help us to know that if you know the truth about your spiritual identity in Christ, you shall be delivered from demonic bondage.

- *Are you in bondage to drugs?*

I declare you free from drugs in the mighty name of Jesus. Amen. Your emphatic Amen shows that you agree with the prayer.

Are you enslaving to alcohol?

Your emphatic Amen shows that you agree with the prayer.

- You are free from alcohol in the mighty name of Jesus

Are you in bondage to perversion?

Amen. Your emphatic Amen shows that you agree with the prayer.

- You are free from perversion in the mighty name of Jesus. Amen. Your emphatic Amen shows that you agree with the prayer.

Chapter 13 : Prayers of Deliverance

- Has the Demons plaque you with the practices of bestiality? Aaamen. Your emphatic Amen shows that you agree with the prayer.

You delivered from bestialism in the mighty name of Jesus. Amen. Your emphatic Amen shows that you agree with the prayer.

- *Are you in bondage to nicotine?* Amen.

Your emphatic Amen shows that you agree with the prayer.

You are free today in the mighty name of Jesus Amen. Your emphatic Amen shows that you agree with the prayer.

- *Are you in chain to fear of men?*

Jesus has free you today in the mighty name of Jesus. Amen. Your emphatic Amen shows that you agree with the prayer.

- Is Satan instigating you to kill your fellow man in the name of religion?

Know Your Spiritual Identity

My God is liberating you today in the mighty name of Jesus. Aaamen. Your emphatic Amen shows that you agree with the prayer.

- ***Are you a Jihadist?***

The truth of is making you free today in the mighty name of Jesus. Amen. Your emphatic Amen shows that you agree with the prayer.

- Are you slaving for false prophets and false Apostles? Amen. Your emphatic Amen shows that you agree with the prayer.

I declare you free from false Christ in the mighty name of Jesus. Amen. Your emphatic Amen shows that you agree with the prayer.

- ***Are you suffering from the result of your sins and perversion?***

Chapter 13 : Prayers of Deliverance

Your sins are forgiven in the mighty name of Jesus. Amen. Your emphatic Amen shows that you agree with the prayer.

- Are you having sex in your dreams?

You are free from spiritual husband in the mighty name of Jesus. Amen. Your emphatic Amen shows that you agree with the prayer.

You are free from spiritual wife in the mighty name of Jesus. Amen. Your emphatic Amen shows that you agree with the prayer.

Prayers to casting out the demonic spirit:

The spirit of perversion, you are cast out in the mighty name of Jesus. Amen.

The spirit of drugs addiction, you are cast out in the mighty name of Jesus. **Amen.**

Know Your Spiritual Identity

The spirit of alcohol, you are cast out in the mighty name of Jesus. Amen.

The wicked spirit of the demon, you are cast out in the mighty name of Jesus. Amen .

Father liberates me from bondage of perversion, cocaine, heroin, nicotine and other vises of the devil, in the mighty Name of Jesus. Amen.

I am free at last, in the name of Jesus. Amen.

Therefore anyone who desires to be free shall be free in the mighty name of Jesus.

Anyone the son has made free, shall be free indeed, in the mighty name of Jesus.

My God and father, Jesus Christ, the sun of righteousness, I bring the readers of this book to the Mount Zion, to your throne of grace, to please use your previous blood and mighty name to wipe out their sins and

Chapter 13 : Prayers of Deliverance

liberate them from their destruction **(Psalm 107:19-20)**.

Deliver them from all forms of perversions. Deliver them from fear and falsehood. Help them to find solutions to their spiritual identity crisis. Help them to develop personal relationship with you. Please Jesus sends your word of healing. Send your word of deliverance, and send your word of salvation in the mighty name of Jesus.

In summary, there is no other time in history, than this period, when Satan the devil has confused the mind of people as to know their own biological and spiritual identity in God. He has blinded the people so much that they did not even know their sexual orientation. Some men are claiming to be a woman after marrying and having children. Some women are marrying their pets, and some men are having sex with animals. The whole world is in darkness, and the gross darkness has covered the people. The confusion has gone beyond social, economic status. It has gone beyond academics, religion, and government. This is what I describe as a spiritual identity crisis. Finding a solution to one spiritual identity crisis is a must for people of God. Otherwise, no one is immune to a spiritual identity crisis. Knowing your spiritual identity is the beginning of wisdom. What went wrong? Satan, the god of this wicked generation, is about to go to Hell and go to prison.

He is desperate to destroy God's children and to depopulate the world. He is using perversions, drugs and alcohol and another form of wickedness to damaged people.

Don't be a victim of the spiritual identity crisis. Finding the solution to the identity crisis is a must for you. Those who did not have Christ in their lives will surely be in crisis.

Chapter 13 : Prayers of Deliverance

This book will revealed to you different ways God is using to reconcile all his children. Knowing Jesus as your savior and the Holy Spirit as your helper will assist you to break free from the vices of the devil. God says, *"My people perish for lack of knowledge, and I will reject their generation for lack of knowledge"*. (Hosea 4:6)

Lack of knowledge will lead to destruction. Knowledge of the truth shall make you free. It is my prayer that after reading this book, "Know your spiritual Identity and The solution to identity crisis" you should be able come to accurate knowledge of the Bible Truth and be loosed from Satanic bondage. God is waiting to welcome you back as God's children.

If you know anyone who is powerless, and cannot help themselves, but have the desire to be free from satanic bondage: We would partner with them to resist the enemy, bind the *powers of darkness* and proclaim victory. Jesus said in Luke 10:19 " *Behold, I give unto you power to tread on serpents and scorpions, and over all the power of the enemy: and nothing shall by any means hurt you"*.

Whatever you bind on earth shall also be bind in Heaven. **(Mathew 18:18)**

Jesus is still healing and delivering people today because Jesus is the same yesterday, today, and forever. I am humble to be a vessel that Jesus is using today.

Read this book entirely two to three times with the Bible references.

Take it like spiritual food every day until you are totally liberated from your afflictions.

Jesus encourage you to share your testimony with us after your healing and deliverance **(Luke 5:13-15)**

Chapter 13 : Prayers of Deliverance

Share your testimony with us

The Global Evangelist: David A Olaniyan
E-mail: jesuswitnessministries@gmail.com
Google: jesuswitnessministries.com
YouTube: JesusWitnessMinistries

Know Your Spiritual Identity

ABOUT THE MINISTRY

Jesus Witness Ministries Inc. is a Bible research organization with emphasis on spreading the good news about Jesus Ransom Sacrifice. JWM is worship center where we worship and honor our creator called, Yahweh, Elohim, Jehovah, God and Jesus Christ our savior and mediator. To build strong faith in the free gift of everlasting life, based on God's grace and favor alone. Your salvation is not due to our hard Work or Self-righteousness (Ephesians 2:7-9 Isaiah 64:5-6).

We believe in the power of Holy Spirit through prayers and fasting. We believe in miracle and in varieties of spiritual gifts. (I Corinthians 12:1-30).

We would answer the call of our savior, Jesus Christ to be his witnesses to all the people and to the most distance parts of the world. (Acts 1:8). We would employed the latest information technology and mass media to accomplish the Lord's work.

We would be diligent to be factual and not to add more to the scriptures or subtract from the Bible as warned by Yahweh, Elohim, Jehovah God in Deuteronomy 4:2, Proverb 6:30 and Revelation 22:18-19. Our teaching will be based on God's word alone.

We would uphold political neutrality of Jesus Christ but will allow individual conscience to dictates to them on political appointment and voting (Galatians 5:1, 13-14).

We strongly believe that our Lord died for all believers and that everyone who has faith in the ransom sacrifice of Jesus have equal chances of being selected to rule with him either in the new earth or in the new heaven. (John 1:12 , 1 John 5:1, Revelation

7:1-15, Revelation 19:1 and Revelation 14:1-3).

We believe that our salvation depends upon partaking of Jesus body and blood in obedience to Him in John 6:41-57. We also believe that 144,000 mentioned in the book of Revelation is symbolic just as their description is symbolic.

We believe that you either belong to Christ, that is, son of God or you belong to the seed of Satan or children of the Devil. (I John 3:9-12; I John 5:1-2; John 1:12) We would uphold the God principles of headship and the Bible principles of one wife and one husband for all our ministers and overseers based on 1 Timothy 3:1-7 and 1 Corinthians 11: 3.

Perhaps most importantly, our members must be familiar enough with the Scriptures to be able to accurately and coherently present the gospel to others. "Always be

Chapter 13 : Prayers of Deliverance

prepared to give an answer to everyone who asks you to give the reason for the hope that you have"(1 Peter 3:15).

Always being prepared means diligent Bible study, memorizing Scripture, and praying for God-given opportunities to share with those whose hearts have been prepared by the Lord to hear His message of salvation.

ABOUT THE AUTHOR

David A. Olaniyan is the founder and the president of Jesus Witness Ministries with headquarters' in East Orange, New Jersey, USA and branch in Lagos and Ogun State, Nigeria.

As a Global Evangelist in high demand, he travels extensively across Europe, Asia and Africa to fulfil the call of God upon his life.

He is an ardent teacher of the word of God. He also operates strongly under the power of the Holy Spirit to bring about salvation, healing and deliverance and revival to the nation of the world. He is a trained Accountant with over thirty years of experience in the gospel ministry. He is happily married with children.